LEADERS DON'T SOLVE PROBLEMS

STUART FRIEDMAN

Leaders Don't Solve Problems

Author: Stuart Friedman
Editor: Matt McGovern
Consultant: Pamela Weinstein, English teacher
Proofreader: Taylor Brien
Cover Design: Melissa Farr, Back Porch Creative
Author Image: Scott Smeltzer Photography
Interior Layout: Griffin Mill

ISBN: 979-8-9881891-4-5

PUBLISHED by CG SPORTS PUBLISHING

AN IMPRINT OF
NICO 11 PUBLISHING & DESIGN
MUKWONAGO, WISCONSIN
MICHAEL NICLOY, PUBLISHER

www.nico11publishing.com

Quantity order requests can be emailed to:
mike@nico11publishing.com

Printed in The United States of America

LEADERS DON'T SOLVE PROBLEMS
Stuart Friedman

TABLE OF CONTENTS

FOREWORD

This book is not a step-by-step guide to becoming a better leader, but it could be a blueprint for immediate impact. It's also not for the faint of heart.

Leaders Don't Solve Problems shares Stuart Friedman's unique philosophy and ideas on ownership, leaders, and how the decisions leaders make to surround themselves with world-class teams (or not) make all the difference between whether their organizations achieve mediocre or exceptional results.

From the trenches to the boardroom, Stuart reveals these principles and perspectives with compelling real-world stories. Each is immediately accessible and relatable. Each is filled with practical insights.

When you step back and look at the success of every world-class organization, at its core there is a leader who has discovered a secret: it is not his or her responsibility to solve problems. These leaders are incredibly rare and fully expect their teams to solve problems before they reach the top. (In fact, imagine if your boardroom was designed to explore and exploit opportunities and crush your competition!)

Unfortunately, even good leaders take too much on themselves and then wonder why they casually volunteered to be the problem solver in the first place. It could be ego; it could be that they have a mediocre team, or it could be there's a poison pill in the boardroom.

1

As a business coach and hall of fame speaker, I have had the privilege of meeting and interacting with professionals all over the world. Stuart is in a category of one. He is incredibly rare and gifted in ways I seldom experience. His ability to listen carefully, see the truth, and cut to the chase on what is happening behind the curtain is profound.

He will provide you with what you need to know and what you'll want to do to achieve the results you **demand** (uncompromised standards, unconditional acceptance). His approach is street smart and brilliant in its simplicity. Engage Stuart to work with your team and facilitate a conversation that holds a mirror up to what your people are doing or not doing and you will never be the same.

In *Leaders Don't Solve Problems,* Stuart weaves his message and magic in a way that can help shine a light on your own unique situation, including the reasons you are the leader you are, who your top performers are and why, and who needs to be left behind. That may sound harsh, but in becoming a world-class organization, you must stop shouldering the responsibility for solving every problem and make sure each member of your team is fully engaged and performing at his or her best. Every. Single. Day.

Mark LeBlanc, CSP, CPAE
2023 NSA Hall of Fame Inductee
Author of *Never Be the Same* and *Growing Your Business!*
Edina, Minnesota

INTRODUCTION

This is NOT a do-it-yourself (DIY), how to "fix" yourself leadership development book. I promise no ideas or suggestions for how to change you or fix you. In my experience, it's not worth your time, effort, or money.

If you are reading this introduction, you're most likely *already* a highly successful leader. So why fix what "ain't broke?" In all likelihood, what got you here *will* continue to get you there.

You may be wondering what I mean by success. I think Maya Angelou said it best with her insightful quote, "Success is liking yourself, liking what you do, and liking how you do it."

That said, even though you *are* highly successful (you should be hearing Maya Angelou's wise words right about now, "Success is liking yourself, liking what you do, and liking how you do it") part of you knows that you and your company could achieve more if only your employees thought about the business like you do—like an "owner."

I call this having an "ownership mindset." It's got nothing to do with stock options, holding a financial stake in the company, or telling people what to do because you're the boss. It's about the people you surround yourself with taking ownership of their roles and being accountable for the decisions they make and the outcomes they achieve or don't achieve. It's about them being excited to come to work every day, stepping into their roles with passion, making stuff happen, and realizing the fruits of their participation.

From your front desk receptionist to your most senior VP, surrounding yourself with people who have an ownership mindset—who are the best versions of themselves every day—is what *will* get you those next level results you desire …that and ascribing to three golden rules for all leaders (more on these "golden rules" later).

Here are some examples of how individuals might think and act like owners:

- A VP of Sales understands the need to increase revenue to ensure bonuses, meet profits for 401K contributions, etc., so she raises prices on products. (Applies initiative aligned with your strategy! You gave her the authority to do this because you trust her ability to think/act like an owner.)

- An analyst owns his research and is thorough, complete, and timely with weekly and monthly reports. He makes himself available before and after meetings to explain the numbers. (Applies initiative aligned with your strategy! You gave him the authority to do this because you trust his ability to think/act like an owner.)

- An administrative staffer gives her all to create a PowerPoint presentation for an important meeting. She's not content with just putting black letters on a white background. How dull and lackluster is that? Even though it's not the primary focus of her job, she wants to do her best to make sure the presentation connects with the audience. (Applies initiative aligned with your strategy! You gave her the authority to do this because you trust her ability to think/act like an owner.)

The bottom line is for owners to let members of their teams do their jobs. After all, leaders don't solve problems, their people do (at least they should). Those owners who have people on their teams who can't do the job, should start the process of moving those people out—if not started already—in favor of employees who are willing, excited, and capable.

Of course, relying on members of the team to do their jobs requires owners who are willing and able to "let go." This can be difficult, especially for owners who prefer to criticize, meddle, and do the work of solving problems themselves.

Even then, this book is not about *how* to instill an ownership mindset in your team. Rather, it's about you as the owner being able to self-examine your personal leadership experiences and explore the experiences of others so you become better able to recognize when having such an ownership mindset on your team could have made (or will make) a difference.

Being a Leader...

You are a leader because of *who* you are, not who you want to emulate or who you might turn into if only you make a few of those changes championed by whatever leadership development book is trending.

You became an effective leader because of all the gifts and assets you bring to the table, such as being visionary, assertive, sociable, passionate, inspiring, driven, etc. You also became an effective leader because of all your blind spots (let's call them "constraints"), such as analysis paralysis, lack of attention to detail, tendency to micromanage, lack of self-awareness, etc.

How could constraints have helped you become a leader? Let's just say the results speak for themselves. You're successful, right? That means you became the leader you are in spite of yourself. You "optimized on your constraints."

I'll come right out and say it: being the best leader you can be has very little to do with fixing or changing you. One of the key aspects of being the best version of yourself is anticipating who you will be communicating with and being empathic to others and to the situation.

How difficult is it to learn to modify your style or approach to the situation—to know what the other person needs to hear and when? Given the typical human aversion to change, apparently it's very difficult!

For example, early in my career I was brought in as a consultant to turn a company's division around. The president gave me three years to make his division profitable. Three years might sound like a long time, but it wasn't. Time flew and eventually we were successful.

The original exit plan was for me to have the option of becoming president of another division in the company once his was turned around. During our three years working together, the president never broached the matter with me, nor did he ever go out of his way to acknowledge any of the successes the team achieved in making his division profitable. Of course, that all changed when I presented him a letter to conclude my engagement. The division was profitable. My job was done.

The president seemed surprised by my letter. "Is there anything I can do? More pay? Stock options?" He asked.

"Why are you asking me only now?" I inquired. "I told you when you signed the engagement agreement three years ago that this day would come and to be prepared. Along the way, there have been plenty of clues this day was approaching. You should have anticipated this, and we should have had this discussion a year ago. I know you thought I was kidding."

One reason good people leave good situations is because leaders fail to communicate and acknowledge contributions in a timely fashion; they fail to anticipate what others need to hear and when they need to hear it.

To Be the 'Ass'... or Not to Be...

There have been leaders who brought me in to work with them and their teams over the years for whom the perceived "ass" inside of them *is* what helped propel them to success. These leaders dangled carrot-sticks, threatened reprimands, bullied, had no self-awareness, and/or showed little empathy for others or their situations.

It wasn't all bad, of course, and being perceived as an "ass" isn't about being right or wrong. After all, that same perceived ass was the one who made all the tough calls, drove results, led the organization forward through thick and thin, and burned the midnight oil when it needed burning.

So, if being perceived as an ass is your leadership "secret sauce," the last thing I want to do is squelch that way of being for you.

For whatever reason, being perceived an ass works for some leaders. Being perceived as an ass is what puts money in their pockets, creates jobs, and pays salaries. It gives them energy to support their drive to achieve and continue to be successful (and we all know what that means, thank you, Maya Angelou!).

Sure, some people may be afraid of such leaders, but that's only because they don't understand how these individuals can be so comfortable with themselves, not needing the validation of others.

Not all leaders are perceived as asses, of course. Some lead by inspiring their teams and setting an appropriate example. They treat people with respect and dignity. They are positive, encouraging, and quick to acknowledge the contributions of others.

But ass or not, the key to effective leadership is being able to *collaborate* and *communicate* effectively in all situations. It's through genuine collaboration that leaders get their teams to think and act like owners, accountable for their particular pieces of the business. With everyone rowing in the same direction, people can solve practically any challenge; they can move mountains.

Of course, not every member of a team will have some of that "ownership" gene inside of them. In small amounts, that's OK. But just remember, for your team to be "world-class" it must be populated with enough people who *do* think and act like owners.

World-Class Team, You Say?

I've never met a leader who didn't want a "world-class" executive team. I define "world-class" as a team whose members step up in situations and make decisions aligned with the leader's strategy, vision, and mission. Members of world-class teams are curious to ask questions when they feel tension, and genuinely want to get the truth out on the table for all to discuss. They routinely go above and beyond. They don't whine if things don't go as planned. Instead, they use the energy others might spend complaining to make things happen. In other words, they perform at their very best every single day—and they're excited about it!

As leader, the people you select to be on your team should supplement and complement all aspects of who you are. For example, if you're not a numbers person, you should have people on the team who are—people who are excited about crunching numbers, drilling down on certain performance indicators, and telling compelling stories through spreadsheets, pie charts, and reports. This allows them to be the best version of themselves, and you to be the best version of yourself.

How you crack the code of building your world-class team ultimately determines how successful your organization can be. While this is not a book about *how* to build a world-class team, know this: no matter your starting point, building a world-class team is possible, it's also necessary for success, and getting there can be an exciting journey.

For example, my first exposure to a prospective client got off to a somewhat dubious start. Walking into the reception area, through a closed door I heard, "F**k you and the horse you rode in on! What the f**k were you thinking? Because that's not what I was thinking!"

I soon learned this seemingly furious individual was the owner of the company. I had never heard an owner talk like this. What was I getting into? Why was he so angry? Was there any hope for this leader and his team?

While there must have been a reason for the outburst, leaders should never let their emotions rule the day—at least not to this extent, and certainly not directed at the team or at individuals in public EVER!

Over the next three months, I worked with this owner and his team to connect the dots between their current situation and what was needed for the team to become world-class. Eventually, they got there. It just took a change in mindset and a willingness by those involved to follow three "golden rules."

Three Golden Rules

To get the most out of your leadership and your team, as a leader you need to do only three things: follow the three "golden rules" for developing a world-class team. That's it.

Simple right?

While they're fairly simple rules, they're not easy to follow.

Golden Rule #1: "Owners/leaders don't solve problems."

Owners/leaders identify issues and give strategic directives to their teams. They surround themselves with people who do the actual work of solving problems and innovating new products and processes—the business decision group—either within their respective departments or for the company as a whole.

It's the leader's role to articulate the organization's direction, vision, or mission and then hand off objectives and goals for the team to solve.

Because an organization's culture starts at the top and then filters down through direct reports to front line staff, getting the team to think and act like "owners" starts with you, the owner. It's your job to get the team to collaborate, create alignment, and solve company issues for the greater good... which brings me to the second golden rule.

Golden Rule #2: "Surround yourself with people who get excited by thinking/acting like owners."

Some people innately want to be the best they can be, day in and day out. They strive to make the most out of every moment and every situation. They get excited. They see potential and opportunity around every corner and with every project. They may not have a financial stake in the business, but they think and act like owners. Whether they're arranging a working lunch for a client meeting or crunching the latest sales numbers for a report to the board, they are accountable.

Others are incapable of thinking like owners. They never get excited. Everything about their work and their role is just another task to get done before they call it a day.

Of course, not every employee can be an A-lister. All companies need a certain percentage of B-players—people who simply come to work and do their jobs each day and do them well.

But when it comes to building a world-class team, who do you want more of?

Golden Rule #3: "Communicate with a high relevance factor."

Winston Churchill once said, "The difference between mere management and leadership is communication"—or more precisely the ability to speak to *how* others listen and vice versa. I call this the "relevance factor."

Whenever you are communicating with other people— whether it's talking, emailing, texting, or even "Zoom"ing—you must modify your communication style and step into a world of empathy where you can hear what those people are saying and you can speak to how they listen. Once you master this skill, what you say, how you say it, and what others hear becomes instantly relevant. It's all about getting your team to hear 100% of your message.

Now, if you're the type of leader who's not willing or able to listen, collaborate, and empathize, then don't do it. If you decide that only your opinion matters, that's great. Stick with the status quo and have a one-sided conversation. It's gotten you this far. Just be sure to set expectations with your team accordingly. (In other words, your team needs to know that when you want their opinion, you'll give it to them.)

You can also choose to sit in your office and not pick up the phone, not compose an email, not text, etc. In fact, you can handcuff yourself so you can't reach your smartphone or computer keyboard. If that sounds like you, then you should adjust *your* expectations accordingly. You're destined to keep achieving the same results you've always achieved, and that may be OK by you.

If either of these scenarios is good enough for you, so be it. Forget about who solves problems. Forget about building a world-class team. Forget about the relevance factor.

Recognize the Signs

There is no judgment as to the type of leader you are. Who am I to judge what got you here? Instead, my mission is to help you see why shifting your paradigm might be the key you need to:

- Get your people to think and act like owners,

- Hire the right people to ensure your legacy thrives,

- Increase revenue momentum, or

- Overcome business challenges that frustrate you.

Again, this is *not* a how-to book. The solutions for every business and leadership challenge are unique. It's a matter of "cut to the chase to find the problem; quick to the truth to find the solution." Solutions come only after *you* are able to recognize there's an issue that needs solving and only after *you* decide to take on the truth of the matter.

If you take a moment to look, the signs are likely all around you:

- Do you have a world-class team?
- Do the members of the team come to work excited each and every day?
- Do they step into their respective roles and make things happen?
- Are they passionate about their roles?
- Do team members think and act like owners?
- What would your business and your results look like if they did?

Following are several real-life scenarios drawn from experiences working with owners, leaders, and their teams (some world-class and some not). These stories, along with lessons learned and heart-felt objectives not met, make up the majority of this book. Each story is based on true events, though I've changed names and certain details to protect the guilty.

By reading these stories, my hope is you can recognize yourself or situations you've been in. How might these scenarios (or your own) have played out differently if those involved thought and acted like owners or were better able to utilize the three "golden rules"?

If you're ready to begin the journey of creating possibility right now, that's *great!* Give me a call at **(312) 543-0013** or email me at stuart@leadersdontsolveproblems.com. If not, I encourage you to read this book and reach out to me afterwards. I look forward to the conversation.

1 | BRING THE BABY TO THE BOARD ROOM

F**k you and the horse you rode in on!"

Those are the exact words I heard shouted from behind a closed door as I walked into the lobby of a prospective client's offices. I will never forget hearing them. They were jarring.

Do people really talk like that in a professional setting?

Moments earlier I had been driving my white SUV, glancing into the rear-view mirror, smiling at the three empty child car seats there, looking forward to when I would pick my boys up later that day, and feeling grateful for the referral to this prospect.

Now I was asking myself, *What the heck am I about to get into?*

Weeks before, I had spoken with the chief executive officer, Pat, to set up this meeting. On that call, Pat came across as efficient, succinct, and no-nonsense. I remember thinking, *That's OK, we can't all be super-sociable types.*

During our conversation, Pat asked about work I had done with similar-sized organizations, like industries, and how I knew the person who referred me. While these were all reasonable questions I got the sense this was Pat's way of letting me know his standards were high. He wasn't going to pick an unknown consultant to work with him and his direct reports. That was fine. He wanted to get the right person and right fit for his company. I embraced the scrutiny.

Pat explained that at our first meeting he would decide whether I was right for the job. I didn't have the heart to tell him that I thought he had this "working together" thing a little one-sided. In my experience, the decision to work together must be mutual—Pat chooses me; I choose Pat—or the relationship won't achieve the desired results.

After the call ended, I had no doubt that Pat was a tenacious, persistent, determined type. Based on my experience, I knew his employees probably perceived him as an "Ass" with a capital "A." That was OK by me. I knew that sometimes leaders were perceived that way and that despite such perceptions, they often became successful anyway.

Let the F-Bombs Fly

As I pulled into the parking lot, I had been thinking about how my communication style needed to be for my meeting with Pat and his executive team. I reminded myself, *Make adjustments so you are direct. Answer their questions efficiently and get to the point without ambiguity.* (Golden Rule #3: "Communicate with a high relevance factor.")

I must admit, though, the very loud "f**k you" I heard when entering the building caught me off guard. Now I could hear the same booming voice screaming again. "What the f**k were you thinking? Because that's not what I was thinking!"

Hmmm…

I paused, took a breath, let it out, and realized the walls separating the lobby from a nearby meeting room must be paper-thin. There were more raised voices. It was nothing distinct, except for a few other curse words that seemed to be part of the same conversation.

Could this be the group of executives I was about to meet?

The lobby consisted of the seating area, where I was standing, and a wall that had a closed door and a sliding-glass-window for greeting people face-to-face. Behind the wall was a counter and a workstation. Behind the workstation was a hallway and those loud voices, seemingly coming from a room somewhere down that hallway.

The lobby had an overall vibe that was more like a doctor's office than a business office. To me, it seemed a bit on the cold, unwelcoming side. I began to wonder if the wall and the closed door was there to keep the inmates in or to keep enemies or visitors out.

The door opened. A woman walked directly toward me. Apparently, my arrival had not gone unnoticed. She reached out for a handshake, introducing herself as Christin. She had a warm, welcoming smile.

Christin explained that she was the CEO's executive assistant. She asked me to have a seat, pointing to several empty chairs. Then she turned, walked back through the door, and disappeared. From my seat, I could not tell where she was headed. I assumed she was going to tell the CEO I had arrived.

No phones?

A minute passed and the yelling started again. A string of F-bombs ensued, carpet-bombing my general vicinity. Whether used as nouns, verbs, or adjectives, the goal of those in the meeting was clear: drop as many F-bombs as creatively and as loudly as possible. Anyone in the lobby or adjoining spaces would have heard the vulgarity, lack of respect, lack of listening, and lack of understanding going on in that meeting.

Christin soon returned to her workstation behind the counter. She opened the sliding window and let me know that the CEO was ready for me to join him and his team. She buzzed me in through the closed door and directed me to the conference room, which *was* at the end of the long hallway.

I passed many individuals at their workstations. Some stared at me as though I had horns on my head, remnants of lunch all over my face, and possibly a booger hanging from my nose. Others stared like they were deer caught in the headlights. Surely these people had heard what I heard. They were situated in a direct line of fire between the lobby and the conference room. What might they be thinking?

Of course, I had no clue what roles any of these people played. Naturally, I was curious but now did not seem like the time to inquire.

Approaching the conference room door, butterflies were starting to get restless in my stomach. This was nothing out of the ordinary. It was a very human reminder for me to get all my senses in-tune and coordinated, and to be prepared for anything.

I took a deep breath, exhaled slowly, and knocked. The door opened almost immediately. A man greeted me by name and introduced himself as Pat, the CEO.

He asked me to take a seat. But where? I gazed around the large, wooden boardroom table and saw my only option was at the other end opposite Pat.

I remember thinking, *what is it with leaders and their penchant for sitting me at the opposite end of long tables?*

I always shower before every meeting. I use deodorant, too. Could this be a subtle way of intimidating the witness?

Present at the table with Pat were four members of his executive team. I later learned they were the EVP of Sales, COO, CFO, and EVP of Information Technology.

There was an awkward silence. Ten eyes bored through me. I wanted to ask if there was a prize for the person who blinked last, but I kept quiet. Of course, the real question was whether I could remain patient, keep my composure, and stay focused long enough so I could find out what was behind all those F-bombs.

I felt like I was playing a child's game.

Suddenly, one of the executives asked, "Who the f**k are you? And what the f**k are you doing here?"

So much for icebreakers.

Pat interjected and explained to his VPs that I was being hired to help the team communicate more effectively, act more respectfully, and be more tolerant. This, he said, would include how team members interacted with each other, within their departments, and with the rest of the organization. His goal was to achieve greater results for the organization and for all employees.

Wait, did he just say I was being hired?

I had talked to Pat once before on the phone and only met him in person minutes ago. This had to have been my easiest selling effort...EVER.

Pat told the group he believed their current way of operating and communicating was a detriment to revenue momentum and incremental profits year-over-year. He said their behavior was preventing other employees from optimizing their talents, which resulted in higher costs per project. Then and there, I understood Pat "got it." Kudos to him for recognizing the need for change.

As I sat and listened, I noticed that none of the individuals, including Pat, were physically intimidating. So I wondered if they were trying to intimidate me with volume and coarse language to make up for their lack of physical stature. I wasn't sure, but I guessed being overly loud and vulgar could be one way to overcompensate versus a show of red Porsches in the parking lot.

The VP who inquired about who I was as an icebreaker, asked if I had any questions.

I wasn't expecting that—at least not yet. I'd only had a brief introduction so far, so expecting me to have questions already seemed premature.

In these kinds of situations, you can either sit back out of concern over protocols, respect, and the right way to do things or you can simply step up to the door of opportunity when it unlocks and push it wide open.

Those who know me can attest that rarely have I ever *not* jumped with both feet into the unknown. Life is more exciting that way.

So, I jumped in with both feet—my whole body in fact—and replied in the affirmative.

"I do have a question," I said. "Do any of you have children or grandchildren?"

At first, they all seemed surprised that I dared to speak, but then, like bobbleheads, they all nodded.

Amazing.

Before he continued, Pat asked me if I had other questions or anything else to say. I told him I did not.

Pat told me he and his team liked to focus on processes and outcomes. He then asked about my process and how many reports they should expect to receive from me. I told him that I did not do reports, that if they wanted reports, I could refer them to a colleague.

"I will conduct a needs-analysis, completed within approximately 30 days," I said. "I will then compose an executive summary, maybe two pages in length, containing problems to solve and suggested action steps for solving those problems. The goal is to cut to the chase to find the problem; quick to the truth to find the solution."

I asked if that would be satisfactory.

I will never forget Pat's response. He said, "It depends. We'll review the summary and then tell you."

I began to suspect this style of retort was Pat's way of "influencing" people to see things and do things *his* way. Essentially, he was telling me, "When I want your opinion, I'll give it to you!" (Later, during the needs-analysis, these suspicions were confirmed. This *was* how Pat dealt with most people in the company.)

I wondered if Pat behaved this way because he felt his people were not thinking/acting like owners of their respective roles and responsibilities—aligned to his mission, vision, and strategy—either because they had never been asked to or they'd never been empowered to.

Blind-Leading-The-Blind Management

Over the next 30 days, I conducted the needs analysis. The first question directed at all executives, directors, and managers was, "What is the most important/valuable asset in this organization?"

Some of the executives answered "people," which was good to hear, though their definition of how people could demonstrate their value was a bit unsettling. "Do as your boss instructs you to do the work," they said. "The way we want you to do the work." What they were really saying—at least how I perceived their words—seemed to be "Do the work or else!"

Most of the other managers and directors identified the "most valuable asset" as their resiliency and ability to take on constant harassment from the executive team, brush it aside, get the work done in a micromanaging environment, and return to work the next day to do it all over again.

Wow!

As I continued the interviews, it became abundantly clear that the employees had no idea how their work impacted the long-term goals of the company, how their work impacted the profitability of any projects, and what the costs were to complete their projects.

That kind of information was shared only after the fact, after a project was done. Then employees would be berated by their bosses—those in supervisory roles below the CEO, starting with the VPs—if the "concealed" project numbers didn't end up where they needed to be.

Another *Wow!*

It became clear to me there was no collaboration, no small group dynamic, nor any efforts or opportunities for project managers to recalibrate while a project was underway. The only strategy evident was for employees to cross their fingers and hope. Their only sense of satisfaction or gratification for a job well done seemed to come in the form of self-acknowledgment and occasional (but certainly not definite) financial remuneration for their successes well after the fact.

In essence, they were managed on the discretionary and conditional model of motivating and inspiring people via implied threat. For Pat and his direct reports, this meant any employees with brighter prospects would leave in a heartbeat if some other company offered to pay more. Who could blame them?

Apparently, this was how Pat and his executives had conditioned all employees, top to bottom. As CEO, Pat would meddle in his direct reports' space, then they would meddle in their respective team members' space, and so on—all in the name of protecting one's assigned margins.

You would think at some point the executives would have mutinied—or at least gotten together and collaborated on each project to determine best practices for optimizing everyone's dollars. To me, it seemed so obvious. But no, the ingrained company culture was one where the executives were all out for themselves. Their mantra was, "Why would I help the person sitting next to me? I did my job. I should get my just due."

Because of this environment, a lot of money was being left on the table, close to an incremental 7% in margin. The CEO wasn't transparent with his thinking about his goals and desires for the organization, though he thought he was being clear. It was no wonder he was prone to outbursts like, "What the f**k were you thinking? Because that's not what I was thinking."

Making things worse, the executives didn't share the owner's goals—what little Pat might share with them—with their own team members. Why so much secrecy? Because this was a privately held company, Pat didn't want his management team to share critical data with their teams. Naturally, that was his prerogative as owner. (Of course, there's a fine line between being reasonably cautious and being so secretive that people can't do their jobs.)

Pat also took pride in the competitive nature of the internal environment he'd created. Why share when you can watch employees undercut each other? His theory was that such a corporate culture would push people to compete to do their best. So what if it was at the expense of others?

Of course, in this sort of environment, there was little if any collaboration for improving processes, systems, procedures, leadership/management approach, or style of communication. There simply were no incentives to do so. It was an "all for one, none for all" mentality.

People spent most of their time in their own heads scheming about how to look like "the hero" to their respective bosses. One of the worst outcomes, of course, was that mistakes were repeated regularly. It was as though each project was brand new. None of the processes, procedures, or best practices were ever documented or shared. That would be like giving the enemy—in this case your teammates—trade secrets only you were privy to.

Cut to the Chase to Find the Problem...

The needs analysis took 30 days as planned, which led to a presentation of recommended next steps to Pat and his team. In those 30 days of observing meetings, team dynamics, and departments, I developed a good sense of how Pat and his executive team impacted the overall performance of the company and its people.

What were those observations? They weren't good.

24

After reviewing the needs-analysis, Pat looked at me and barked, "Two pages? Really? That's it? My whole organization? You make a declaration about our challenges and what we must do to improve revenue momentum and it's all of two pages? I'm paying you all this money for two pages?"

Looking Pat straight in the eye, without hesitation, I said, "You can pay for the two pages immediately and I will exit right now. It was great to meet you and your team. Or you can all re-read the two pages, ponder what they say, and then reach out to me to discuss where to go from here. It's your choice."

Two days later, Pat called. He asked me to come back for another meeting. He and his team wanted to discuss moving forward.

If you're keeping score:

- **Home Team** (irrationally angry CEO) = 0 points
- **Visiting Team** (poised, calm consultant with the truth) = 1 point

The essence of the needs-analysis did indeed "cut to the chase" for Pat and his team. Here were the main points:

- **Culture:** if the CEO yells at one of the direct reports, that executive will then yell at his or her direct reports, and so on. It's like an abusive and perverse game of dominoes.
- **Management Style**: Command and demand. Indemnify and blame.
- **Recommendations for CEO:**

    - Put more insulation in the walls and ceilings to create sound proofing.

    - Say "please" and "thank you."

    - Eliminate the vulgarity.

- Smile when you're with people or don't be with people.

- Share financial goals with all departments and allow them to use their expertise to optimize on the constraints.

- Allow for collaboration on projects across silos rather than blaming across silos.

Challenge Accepted, Game On

When I next met with Pat and his VPs, we were back in the meeting room with the paper-thin walls. Nothing was said as I headed to "my" chair at the end of the table opposite Pat.

As I settled in and made eye contact, Pat told me he was "disgusted by such a measly report, only two pages." He then literally threw the document at me and said, "This report is juvenile at best. I was expecting a thorough report, with charts, diagrams, and graphs."

Holding eye contact with him, I repeated what I previously shared: "I don't do reports. If you want reports, I'll make a referral to a consultant who does."

Pat turned red. His veins bulged. The looks on the faces of his minions reflected shock and amazement. I could only guess that no outsider—maybe not even an insider—had ever dared talk to Pat that way.

He regained his composure quickly. He asked me what I would tackle first.

"Normally I start by working with the CEO one-on-one," I said. "But given the response to my report, I would prefer to take on the *entire* executive team concurrently."

With a smug grin, Pat asked if I meant all at once.

"It will be the team as a whole, not individually," I said.

26

Pat and I met alone after this meeting. He seemed intent to continue trying to intimidate me. "If you can get my team not to use vulgarity in the next meeting, I will pay double your fees for the initial phase and we will create an engagement for working together going forward," he offered.

"Challenge accepted," I countered, to show him I was a mensch. "When I am successful, we're successful...and I get to choose the charity you'll donate the extra fees to."

Self-assuredly, Pat agreed. I could tell he figured he couldn't lose.

This brief encounter clarified much of my thinking about Pat:

- He reinforces, encourages, and invests in his bad behavior.

- He wants to be right, and he dares people to prove otherwise.

- Many people are "sheeple" and subject to herd-mentality, letting the "Pats" of the world intimidate them. For them, work and life are easier, with less effort. Those who are agreeable to doing what they're told gain a false sense of security.

- Pat bets *against* his desired goal. It's almost like self-sabotage. It's as though he needs to create problems so he can solve them to feel good about being the CEO—to feel like he's the smartest guy in the room.

...Quick to the Truth to Find a Solution

Our next meeting was the following week. I had negotiated for it to be held on a specific day of the week. It was also when monthly financials were due. Surely there would be heated discussions about sales, expenses, projects, and more.

Instinctively, I knew Pat was setting me up for failure. He wanted to prove how smart he and his team were and how unsuccessful I would be using my methods.

What a plan—hire, invest in a consultant, then aim for failure!

The circumstances for this meeting were prime for more F-bombs, disrespect, and the other bad behaviors I had come to associate with Pat and his "world-class" team. It was apt to be like the shootout at the O.K. Corral—only no guns, just bullets of vulgarity.

At this early juncture in my relationship with Pat and his direct reports—it was only my third face-to-face meeting with the whole team—I was not yet invited to their entire meetings. Pat had informed me beforehand that I would be joining the meeting in progress after they had covered financial results.

Entering the lobby, I noticed Christin seemed less self-assured than in our previous encounters. Her shoulders were slumped; her head was down. Sure enough, F-bombs were already being lobbed from the conference room. I asked Christin if she felt this kind of behavior—the tone of voice, the crudeness—was acceptable. "No," she said. "But I'm afraid if I say anything, I'll lose my job."

I asked if she ever expressed her discomfort to the CEO.

She replied "yes" and shared that the behavior had improved for about a week. But as though they couldn't help themselves, the inappropriate conduct of Pat and his team had returned.

I thanked Christin for being so candid.

As I approached the conference room door, I stopped for a moment so I could listen.

Suddenly, the volume level dropped to near normal, yet I could still hear what was being said. Pat was telling the team about his bet with me. The response from the VPs was predictable: "No f**king way," "He's an idiot, a moron," "This person will get chewed up and spit out," and "I say he's gone within 15 minutes of walking in."

I knocked on the door and someone inside told me to enter. As usual, my empty chair awaited at the end of the table opposite Pat. Without hesitating, I headed straight for it, paying close attention to the body language and behavior of Pat and his team. Their eyes bulged as if they'd seen a ghost. Their mouths were agape. They suddenly sat up straight, hands folded on the table, on their best behavior.

I had gotten their attention.

What triggered this changed behavior immediately when I entered the room?

A. Did I take out a loaded pistol?

B. Did I flash "photos" of the executive team in compromising situations?

C. Did I play a recording of past conversations implying they could be sued?

D. A, B

E. A, C

F. B, C

G. All the above

H. None of the above

If you selected "H," none of the above, you have earned yourself a complementary 30-minute consultation. Please contact me at (312) 543-0013 or stuart@leadersdontsolveproblems.com.

Defusing Their F-Bombs

The day I chose for the meeting was "Bring Your Child to Work Day."

To win the bet and make the impact needed so that Pat and his team would be open to my recommendations, I had to get at least one child into that conference room. (Adults change their behavior instinctively around babies. It's part of the human condition and I had three young sons, so…)

As I entered the room, I went straight to my regular perch opposite Pat. Before taking a seat, I placed a sleeping baby, seat and all, atop the table.

What do you think went through the minds of Pat and the executives when they saw the child? A few tears welled up in the eyes of a couple of them, so I'm thinking they felt shame and embarrassment—and maybe a little disappointment in how they'd behaved. At that moment, they must have recognized exactly who they were and how inappropriate their conduct had become.

Knowing they each had children or grandchildren, I had gambled that none would continue to spout obscenities and raise their voices to bully, intimidate, and influence in the presence of a child.

For anyone still keeping score, let's do a quick update:

- **Home Team** (Pat & the VPs) = 0 points
- **Visiting Team** (me) = 2 points

I also hoped this would force them to look inward and be more receptive to the paradigm shift in their ways of working and communicating suggested by the needs-analysis.

- **Home Team** = 0 points
- **Visiting Team** (me) = 3 points

So, I handed all two pages of the "juvenile and measly" executive summary to them for review again. I also handed the CFO an invoice for *double* the mutually agreed upon fee, payable upon receipt.

He glanced at Pat. I suspected he was looking for some sort of indication as to what he should do—accept the invoice or tear it up. With no obvious signal from the CEO, the CFO took matters into his own hands—apparently, *he* could think and act like an owner—and phoned the controller. He asked that a check be written and ready for signature within 10 minutes. (Golden Rule #2: "Surround yourself with people who get excited by thinking/acting like owners.")

Pat didn't say a thing. We just sat for what proved to be an awkward 8 to 10 minutes watching the baby sleep, unaware of all the drama surrounding him or the impact he was having on a room full of adults.

Within 10 minutes, the check arrived. To lighten the mood, I dropped it on one of its longer edges, acting as though it might bounce. It did not—and the CFO chuckled.

The After Picture

I ended up working with Pat and his company for several years. During that time, the company doubled in size. The key was implementing a "small group dynamic" approach within all levels of the organization, from Pat and his direct reports to the VPs and their direct reports, all the way down to each supervisor and manager.

To get people to perform well, everyone at every level needed to start thinking and acting like owners of their respective roles—excited to be there, contributing their best every day, and being recognized for their valuable efforts.

They needed to treat one another with respect and to learn to collaborate and share best practices companywide. They needed to be a world-class team, not only in name but through their actions.

Once we started to build momentum, I was no longer intimately engaged in the guidance and development of the small group dynamic. Once that way of work and of being became self-sustaining, I was able to focus my attention on other ways for Pat to mentor and coach his direct reports so they could mentor and coach their direct reports, and so on down the line.

It took a while, but we got there. As they say, "Rome wasn't built in a day."

The answer for Pat and his team had been obvious. If you want revenue growth and momentum—whatever your desired outcomes might be—you must show respect, foster collaboration, be tolerant, and openly support the people whose job it is to achieve those things for you...and then let them do it. Remember, leaders don't solve problems. Pat and his executive team just needed a nudge.

Why should it have taken such an extreme action to get a little dignity, honor, and respect? I don't know. I'm not a psychiatrist or a psychologist—though at the time I felt like I had gained a little insight into what Jean Valjean from *Les Misérables* must have felt!

Just chalk it up to a "win-win-win-win-win-win" situation for everyone involved:

- CEO = win
- Employees = win
- Company = win

- Clients/Customers = win

- The Charity = win

- Humble Consultant = win

Golden Rule #1: "Owners/leaders don't solve problems."

Golden Rule #2: "Surround yourself with people who get excited by thinking/acting like owners."

Golden Rule #3: "Communicate with a high relevance factor."

Contact STUART FRIEDMAN:

stuart@leadersdontsolveproblems.com | (312) 543-0013

---

2 | THE SINS OF TREATING PEOPLE LIKE NUMBERS

To complete a lengthy project overseas, I was away from home for about seven months, with no return visits, not even for a weekend. When I finally did get back to the USA, adjusting to thinking and acting "like an American" took about two days.

To speed up re-acclimation, some colleagues and I decided to get together so we could catch up on what happened while I was away. We all agreed to take the next Friday as a personal day and meet at our favorite restaurant where the owner knew us, the cooks knew our nuanced palates, and the waitress would put up with our antics.

We arrived promptly at 7:00 a.m. to the aroma of crappy diner coffee. My colleagues and I greeted each other, the owner, the cook, and the waitress and we took our seats at our "reserved" table. I made a point of *not* sitting at one end of it.

Without hesitation, the office gossip started: "Did you hear about this project?" and "Did you hear that so-and-so got engaged, and this one got married, and this one got divorced?" and "Did you hear about this new client?"

Adam, an executive-advocate of mine, looked straight at me, trying to catch my glance. Once our eyes locked, his stare went right through me. Adam had a certain way of speaking that made you feel like there was no one else in the world except you and him. As he spoke, the sounds of conversation, laughter, clinking dishes, and clattering silverware all disappeared.

Adam described an overseas project that was running behind schedule and over budget. He said he'd heard my name floated by top management as someone who could take over the effort and possibly right the ship. Adam also said he considered the job to be "career-limiting" because of all the dysfunction and was worried that I was being offered up as a potential sacrifice.

At this particular point in my career, I had never been asked to step into an ongoing project and get it back on track. I had always been involved with startups and new client projects. If offered, this would be new territory for me, an opportunity too good to refuse.

As Adam continued to share, butterflies started to dance in my stomach (and I'm pretty sure it wasn't because of the coffee or food). What did this mean for me and my future with the company? Was this a chance for me to create possibility and build credibility…or would it truly be career limiting?

I knew wondering about it was a huge waste of energy, so I shook my head and re-entered the present, listening to all Adam had to say.

Pomp and Circumstance, but No Profitability

Two weeks after my conversation with Adam, I received "The Invitation" from several higher ups to attend a project meeting related to an international client.

Wanting to look the part of a confident individual ready for whatever might come his way, I arrived about 10 minutes early. For me, that's called being on time—plus it gave me a few moments to make sure I had no coffee stains on my tie and that my shirt was tucked-in.

The conference room I walked into was unlike any I had ever seen. The room was filled by an elegant, richly-toned wooden table surrounded by 12 luxurious, high-back leather chairs.

In attendance were the company's managing stakeholder and its senior executive. Both were long in stature and clout. They sat at one end of the table. To their right was a junior executive, the #2 person on the project, responsible for overall project management. To the left of the senior executive was another junior executive, #3 on the project, who was responsible for technology management. To the right of the #2 was the senior client manager, responsible for maintaining staffing for the project, and to the left of the #3 was another senior client manager, responsible for managing the specifics of the budget.

I must admit to being awestruck and a little intimidated. I had never met any of these people but had heard stories about their notorious behavior.

Asked to sit at the opposite end of the table—nothing new there—I nodded and made my way to my assigned seat. As I walked, I tried to size up my position relative to all this pomp and circumstance.

Why are they asking for me? What do I bring to the table?

I knew my technical background differed from what was needed on this project. I was not yet experienced in project profitability and managing budgets at this scale.

What if they have questions I can't answer?

I remember having a flashback to my father speaking to me. He would always criticize me for not hearing/listening to my mother or to him. He would say we were gifted with two ears and one mouth to listen twice as much as we talk. It was sage advice then and sound advice now, so I decided to play humble, respectful, and honorable to the other attendees. They probably didn't give a crap about what I had to say anyway. This was bound to be one of those situations where, if they wanted my opinion, they would give it to me.

A project summary and analysis report was distributed, but since I was at one end of the table, I had to get up and walk back to "them" to get my copy. I figured this was a way for them to ensure I knew my place. I was their subordinate, and they expected me to acquiesce.

Quickly glancing at the report, I determined it to be the financials for the international project. Before I could even return to my chair, the senior executive started barking proclamations and declaring absolutes. His tone made it obvious to all in attendance that he was in charge of this project. It was also clear that he wasn't speaking to me but to his "world-class" team.

Proclaiming the objective for the project—profitability!— he sounded frustrated and weary, as though he'd done this kind of thing a hundred times before. He was not pleased with the results to date nor any of the proposed solutions, nor was he happy to be looking at added expenses in the form of a person (me) to help solve the problem. Not to mince words, he was upset, and he expected the team to figure out a way to incorporate the additional cost of me and still come out at or above the profitability target. (Golden Rule #1: "Owners/ leaders don't solve problems.")

Way to really diminish my worth as a human being, I thought. *I'm nothing more than a barrier to profitability!*

At the same time, I found myself grateful for his truth and candor. I had never heard a high-level executive speak with such transparency.

Ignorant, Unambiguous Judgment

I reviewed the project data for a few minutes and began to see trends in the numbers. They were not good trends. The numbers were not only less than optimal, they were abominable. All project activities were behind schedule and over budget.

About 30 minutes into the meeting, the senior executive stood up and looked directly at me, using what I interpreted to be his best "good ol' boy stare-down to intimidate the young guy" technique. I was expecting this, so I stared right back at him. Finally, he officially welcomed me to the team by speaking my last name out loud. He said he expected to see me three months from then with a plan to achieve stated objectives and meet profitability goals.

Of course, I knew the stated objectives included me solving for how to make up for the additional fees and "incremental expense" related to my involvement.

I got it. He was a leader who got results with his own approach and style. Who was I to judge? He was who he was, and it worked. It was nothing personal. He wanted me to be accountable.

To him, though, I imagined my "brand" would be forever tainted because of my potential impact on his profitability. I must have seemed like a symbol of fewer dollars in his pocket—the evil necessary to correct course, the incremental expense that would bias his opinion of me from that point forward even if results were stellar.

I sensed that we would get along. We would never become BFFs, and that was OK. What I liked is that he was clear and unambiguous.

When he gave an assignment, made a request, or delegated a task, he expected one of three responses:

1. "Yes sir. I understand and will get it done. Anything else?"

2. "I don't understand. Here are my questions. Can you please answer them, or can we discuss further?"

3. "I don't agree with your approach. Here is an alternative and this is why I think this is a more optimal approach."

What was not acceptable was no response. That was the kiss of death.

Most importantly, this leader helped introduce NMP ("Not My Problem") into my vernacular. It's a simple phrase that has stuck with me to this day.

After declaring I had three months to come up with a plan, the senior executive left the room. Most other members of the team hung around for about 30 seconds, then they exited. There were no "thank-yous" and no "good lucks." They just left, except for the #2 on the project. He stood, told the others he would catch up, and asked me to stay behind.

Was I about to be brought into the inner sanctum?

The #2 politely welcomed me to the team and told me plane tickets would be sent to my office. He also said I would be staying at a hotel for my first three months. He didn't want to put me into anything more permanent until I proved myself. He explained how I was simply the "pony" on which the team had placed its bets. None of them knew if I was going to fail or save them.

"This project will either make or break my future at this firm," he told me. "Do you want to know why *you* were asked to take on this job?"

I nodded. Of course I wanted to know.

Expecting some sort of accolades or pep talk, he instead told me I was "essentially the goat" (and by this he did not mean "greatest of all time") should the project fail. "You're my buffer and if you f**k up, I can still move up because it will be your ass, not mine."

Wow! So much for the inner sanctum. Welcome to the big leagues, son.

"This is where the rubber meets the road," he told me. "I wish you luck."

At least he was being unambiguous.

I could have been appalled, but instead I felt grateful, energized even. I knew where I stood and what was expected. Not everyone can say that, at least not professionally. I was being gifted the opportunity to act and think like an owner— and it was an opportunity I wouldn't dream of refusing.

Bold but Cocky, Pompous, and Arrogant

From information gleaned in several documents distributed at the meeting, I knew only a handful of details about the project so far:

- The client operated in a country that was an ally of the United States.

- The project was a showcase effort for the organization on a grand scale.

- If the project achieved its objectives, many doors of opportunity would open for the senior executives.

- The project was designed to prove the organization could play in any country's backyard regardless of location. It was to be a testament to the organization's ability to recruit and train superior talent, develop managers, collaborate internationally, and foster a deep and diverse culture companywide.

As I would soon learn as the project unfolded, the words "on track" were salient to my success. Every managing executive, whether senior or junior, was concerned about whether the project was on track. To them, being on track meant keeping the project profitable, which equaled more bonus dollars in their pockets.

Got it!

One attribute of the company was its willingness to take on risk. It's one of the reasons I chose to work there. The unspoken motto was "the higher the risk, the higher the reward." The company recruited well, trained well, and developed client managers well.

My new project had high risk-tolerance written all over it as imagined by the bold executives who negotiated the initial deal. Unfortunately, as bold as they were, these particular managing executives were also devoid of vision. They failed to anticipate the various what-if scenarios that could, and probably would, inevitably manifest. Instead, their only focus was on the basic business modeling and planning tools needed to complete the project.

I do not believe these individuals ever asked, "What happens if?" or "What are the barriers to success?" They probably entered the project design phase as cocky, pompous, and arrogant. It was just another consulting project like so many already in the company portfolio—same old, same old.

Flight Into the Unknown

On my nine-hour flight overseas, I dug into the project data, trying to familiarize myself with trends in the numbers and what they meant for the project and my job. I also read up on all the players involved.

The members of the project management team had at least four or five years of tenure with the company. They were experienced. I wasn't dealing with newbies.

As I became more familiar with the project, I realized I could do this my way. I was accountable and had nothing to lose. If I didn't get the results the senior executive and the #2 on the project desired, I'd be fired. That was pretty obvious.

If I *did* get the desired results and somehow saved their asses, I might not be fired, but I wouldn't be getting a ticker tape parade either. I might have been less experienced, but I wasn't naïve enough to think they would feel indebted to me or grateful. With this company, credit was rarely passed on to those who deserved it. Whoever was in charge—the senior executive in this case—and maybe the number two guy would get all the kudos.

But would the solution be what the senior executive and his team wanted to hear? Should it matter to me whether they wanted to hear it or not? (After all, if something needs to be said, I say it—not to be negative or just to be heard, but to be constructive.)

Arriving at the project venue, the onsite management team— my new colleagues for at least the next three months—greeted me warmly. They seemed happy to see me, perhaps because I was a new face and someone they might grow to trust. I was also sure, based on how my company typically worked, they assumed I had an immense amount of experience.

What's that famous saying, "When you assume, you make an ass out of 'u' and me?"

Hmmm…

Cut to the Chase to Find the Problem…

I hit the ground running with a 3-month plan in hand.

Month One

- Locate the low-hanging fruit (quick hits).
- Complete a needs analysis (take a pulse of the overall environment/project, cultural influences).
- Study the small group dynamic.
- Discover what the team thinks is needed with respect to:
  - Current role descriptions.
  - Expectations.
  - Metrics.
  - Resumes (internal).
  - Talent/what people love to do and how this impacts profitability.

- What does the staff reporting into the onsite management team think? What do they think really matters? What do they think really works?

- What does the organizational chart look like for the 60 people who comprise the onsite team (other than management)?

Month Two

- Increase communication effectiveness. (Golden Rule #3).

  - Start to break down communication barriers between the client management team (back at home) and the onsite management team.

  - Begin breaking down communication barriers between the onsite management team and its direct reports.

- Gather more data about people, in particular their respective biases related to their current peers/colleagues on the job. Determine their expectations about:

  - Job role clarity and outcomes, their participation.

  - Compensation.

  - Time off.

  - With whom they would be working.

Month Three

- Create an executive report for the client management team outlining current challenges to:

  - Profitability (being on time and on budget).

  - Alignment to strategy.

  - Various behaviors and outliers.

After three months of living in a foreign country and adapting to its culture, I gained insights related to why this project was failing. My needs analysis revealed:

- The team consisted of people representing four different nationalities, cultures, and/or countries.

- There were no onboarding efforts to integrate the team to understand perspective, discuss expectations, or learn about each other.

- The onsite management team was ill-equipped to understand the communication barriers between the people onsite, not just in terms of language but also cultural meanings and sensibilities.

- There was little desire for people to connect with others assigned to this project outside of their nationality or country.

- None of the onsite managers stepped up to lead the effort to grow team cohesiveness.

- All members of a respective country worked in their own silos, forming cliques based on nationality. This resulted in four "fully staffed" teams of individuals. Consequently, if a programmer on team "Country A" reported to a manager from "Country B" on paper, the programmer might go to the manager of "Country A" (same country) with a question instead. The manager from "Country A" wouldn't necessarily know the requirements for the manager from "Country B," so guesswork prevailed.

- Through their actions and job performance, no one below the level of the client management team seemed to care about the greater good, the client, or any contractual agreements.

- Onsite, there was no accountability, no curiosity, and total intellectual apathy. Blame was passed around as quickly as a hot potato.

- People from countries who tended to make less than people from other countries stayed in lower cost housing.

I could go on (and on), but you get the picture. This was a case of near total dysfunction. However, knowing the truth and the remedy didn't make my job presenting the findings in terms of "profit, profit, profit" any easier. The client management team wanted to hear the "dollar story" and how I was going to recoup profits lost to date, which at this juncture was six months into the overall contract.

With nothing to lose and staying true to my irreverent self, I *would* tell the leaders what they probably didn't want to hear.

...Quick to the Truth to Find a Solution

As previously arranged, at the end of my time overseas, I returned home. Sitting in a small waiting area outside the main conference room where this journey began, I watched as the five people I had met before walked by. Soon, they were joined by three others in the conference room and the door closed. No one bothered to invite me in. I doubted it was an oversight. Clearly discussions were being held above my paygrade.

About 20 minutes later, the door opened. The junior executive, #2, invited me in.

I'd be lying if I said I wasn't nervous, but I *was* mentally and physically prepared. Anticipating this meeting for weeks, what I couldn't have known was *who* I spied sitting at the other end of the conference room table. It was *the* boss, the head honcho of the company—the senior executive's boss.

Pleasantries were exchanged, if you can call them that. It was a poor attempt to cut the tension. As I took my seat, I noticed everyone but the senior executive was looking down at the table immediately in front of them. Mimicking them, I looked down and then looked *underneath* the table.

The top boss asked what I was doing. I explained how I wasn't sure if there was something I was missing because almost everyone else was looking under the table. He did not seem impressed or in the least bit amused by my response.

Nevertheless, he thanked me for my executive summary but stated he was expecting something much more thorough and in-depth than what I delivered.

"As far as I'm concerned, your report is incomplete," he said.

Reminding myself that I had nothing to lose (at least that was the thought at the time), I chose to be my irreverent self.

I said to *the* boss that the summary actually was the supplement/complement to all the financials for the project that were supplied by the client management team the day before, which had the usual project financials but little to no insight related to the team, the people.

"You should have expected more from the client management team," I explained, deciding at that moment to go for it. After all, I knew these people liked a fight, so I decided to give them a fight on their terms.

The boss asked me why I felt that way.

"When you run a project of humans based on numbers only, the only thing you can do is fail," I shared. "People are not made of numbers. They create the numbers, such as production time, deliverable accuracy, hours worked, and more. The financials are actually lag indicators of what has already happened, not an indication of what is going on and certainly not predictors for future performance. By the time you got a look at the numbers, it was too late—the reports were already out of date."

I argued (constructively, of course) that they needed to put the numbers aside and discuss the team. In my opinion, the client management team was ill-equipped to deal with people who were not like them. They were intolerant. But this was not about being right or wrong, good or bad. The client management team just didn't know. They simply refused to connect with the people from parts of the world who weren't like them because they didn't think they had to. But they could all speak English and, with minimal effort, they could have built rapport with the overseas team, allowing them to feel good about being on the project and, more importantly, being a part of this great organization (Golden Rule #3).

"Right now, the onsite team is in a free-for-all downward spiral," I continued. "It will take at least three to six months to see a change in overall results."

Seemingly intrigued, *the* boss pushed me on this perspective. He wanted to know how I could be so sure about the turnaround in results.

"I made a deal with all the onsite team members," I said. "I took the onsite management team aside and told them exactly what we'd do when I returned from this meeting."

- All members at the client site would live in the same level of housing regardless of income level.

- A small group dynamic would be formed to create an onboarding process to make everyone feel safe and included.

- I would work with the onsite project managers to develop their skills to work with people from countries other than their own.

What I asked from them in return was a three-month commitment to stay on the project. I suggested they wait to see the results of my meeting back in the USA. If after three months, and if my recommendations had been implemented, then—and only then—if they were still inclined to quit, they could quit. I would even help them exit with confidence to find their next job.

The boss was fuming. He turned red, veins bulging in his forehead. Either I had beat him to the punch, made commitments beyond my paygrade, or he was still stuck in the paradigm that money could solve all problems.

Had the "people" aspect of my argument registered?

"What are all these rumblings I've heard about inequitable compensation, about people from one country earning more than people from another country?" He asked.

Rumblings? As far as I knew there were no rumblings. Was this a last-ditch effort by the boss to steer the conversation away from people issues, which would take time to fix, to seemingly more cut-and-dried issues around money and compensation?

While overseas, I had asked everyone if the salaries they were receiving were what they expected. Across the board, they all answered with a resounding and unanimous "Yes!" I also asked if they knew people from other countries who might be earning more. Again, their response was united and emphatic: "Yes!" Compensation clearly wasn't the issue. There was no dissatisfaction about pay.

What I really wanted to ask the boss was, "Where did you hear that BS? If there are any rumblings about compensation, it's not true." Instead, I explained how the issue of inequitable compensation had been resolved without promising any salary increases. The focus needed to be on the team dynamic.

"People don't resign due to money unless an outside offer is outrageous," I explained. "They leave because their bosses, usually their immediate boss in particular, are disrespectful, dismissive, or ungrateful—much like the client management team sitting at this table."

The boss wanted to know if I would be comfortable continuing to work with these disrespectful, dismissive, ungrateful individuals.

"Of course," I said. "They're the ones who allowed me to participate and contribute to the success of this project. They're a gift to me. I have learned quite a bit from them. They represent an example of human beings I choose not to emulate…ever."

The boss turned to the client management team and asked if they had anything to say in response to my presentation.

Everyone looked to the senior executive for his response.

"It's clear," he said. "That Friedman needs to remain on this project and help the team get this back on track."

The boss agreed, looked at me, smiled, and declared, "Friedman, I don't know where you get your chutzpah from. You are a valuable asset with incredible insights about people. I'm grateful and I'm sure in time this client management team will be just as grateful, probably in three months when we start seeing the results of your work.

"I have thoughts about your future here," he continued. "As long as you're willing to step into high-risk situations and be irreverent to obtain results, you will be a part of this company.

I'm already thinking about your *next* four to five assignments. Thank you, Friedman. And, by the way, I want you to call me directly at the end of each week with pertinent updates: financials with culture."

We All Kept Our Word

The next several months went as envisioned. The client management team expended energy during this second phase into all the areas they hadn't before. They focused on equitable housing, fostering a small group dynamic, creating an onboarding process that was inclusive and respectful, and training and development for new skills and improving old ones.

Of course, the first month of phase two was the worst— again, as expected. The difference was the onsite team and the client management team could see light at the end of the proverbial tunnel (and they knew it wasn't hitched to the front of a locomotive). A month of getting worse before it got better was needed for the dust to settle from the nonsense during the project's initial phases.

By the second month after meeting with *the* boss, we were finally getting back on track. The numbers were trending positive in most categories. More importantly, the people were at ease, engaging with each other and doing a better job of collaborating. Knowing they were satisfying the client, their respective bosses, and themselves seemed to boost their positive energy. They felt valued and purposeful. They were excited to come to work and do a good job every day (Golden Rule #2).

At the end of phase two, the project results were nearly on track to reach all original financial objectives. I remained on the project for a total of nine months.

At the conclusion of my engagement, the senior executive asked me to join him in his office. He simply said, "Thank you for your contribution" and then dismissed me. I thanked him for the opportunity.

Subsequent to this project, *the* boss honored his word. I stayed an additional four years at the company, traveling the world, opening new offices in foreign countries. One of the highlights was leading a joint startup with a software company where we recorded $350 million in sales in the first year.

Of course, Adam was right. Despite my success, my brand never fully recovered. It might have seemed unfair at the time, but looking back now, it turned out OK.

Golden Rule #1: "Owners/leaders don't solve problems."

Golden Rule #2: "Surround yourself with people who get excited by thinking/acting like owners."

Golden Rule #3: "Communicate with a high relevance factor."

Contact STUART FRIEDMAN:
stuart@leadersdontsolveproblems.com | (312) 543-0013

3 | SALES VS. SERVICE: BUSINESS AS USUAL

When the approval process for agreeing on an engagement and moving forward becomes long and arduous, all parties become frustrated—perhaps even a little annoyed.

For one such engagement in particular, there were several times over its course that I thought, *Screw this! Is this organization, and more specifically the president of the division, truly interested in growing and enhancing the employee experience in order to impact the client experience …or not?*

Of course, this really wasn't anything new.

So often during my journeys to and from corporate offices over the years, I have found myself asking, "Is this going to be an exercise in formality and perceptions versus a substantive discussion of what really matters, like revenues, margins, and people?" Usually, it has been the former.

This engagement was with an organization of approximately 10,000 employees. Their process for bringing someone on board as a third-party/consultant was similar to hiring an employee at the executive level. It included a series of interviews with various other executives.

I was asked to participate in seven interviews over eight weeks with five flights to and from various company venues. After the interviews, Thomas, the division president, retained me to lead efforts to turn his division around. He gave me the same authority as a senior VP: decision-making for hiring, discretion for distributing budgeted dollars, investments in people, bonuses, etc. (Golden Rule #2).

Cut to the Chase to Find the Problem...

Thomas shared various insights about his division, which had clients employing up to 125 people. His division was sucking wind, experiencing a 42% client turnover rate and 34% employee attrition—both of which were all-time highs (or should I say lows?).

With results like that, Thomas didn't need to show me any financials. The only thing those reports would do is reinforce their failure to date and continue the negativity. (There's a famous quote about doing the same thing over and over and expecting different results. *Hmmm?*)

At the outset of the engagement, Thomas introduced me as a "change agent" to his management team. This team consisted of the directors of sales, service, HR, operations, and technology. I liked the change agent moniker primarily because it did not categorize me by describing my services. This made me hopeful people would not assign stereotyped perceptions and biases. I was brought in to make a difference, to do things differently, to bring about change.

Thomas told me he felt someone from the outside would have a greater chance to make an impact versus a tenured individual with the company, especially since the average length of employment with staff in his division was 12 years.

The journey, he explained, would be one of transformation for a business that had been around for decades. (I remember thinking, at the time, that his words about transformation were music to my ears. He seemed on top of things!)

When Thomas and I agreed to terms for this engagement, one of the key provisions was that once work was completed and objectives met, he would have me join the organization's executive team as the president of another division. Thus, my joining the organization was a possibility the engagement called for us to discuss annually.

When introduced to his team, they did not greet me with exuberance or any semblance of excitement. Some seemed barely able to muster enough energy to shake my hand. Those who did shake my hand, did so weakly. I was disappointed.

The word "change" does funny things to people, I thought. *No one really likes change. Maybe that's it.*

My energy level coming into this engagement was high, so I chose not to waste time and good energy pondering reasons for their lack of enthusiasm.

Thomas shared with the team that I was brought on board to help implement change in "how we do business" and to drastically increase both employee and client retention. The goal was to increase revenues and margins and plant the seeds for greater recurring revenue from existing customers.

He asked his direct reports to share what was top of mind for them: what was working, what was not working, what they would keep doing, stop doing, what they would change, and finally what they would start doing. Sales and service— especially how each of those areas impacted client turnover— became the consensus for what the team said needed the most attention.

Within the first 90 days, I conducted a needs analysis of the division. I held in-depth conversations with all management team members, gathering input based on the strategy Thomas provided. Whenever discussions turned to the possibility of changing things that were not working or how the organization might implement new ideas, the most frequent comments shared were, "that's not how we do things here" and "we've never done it that way before."

The resistance to someone from the outside was staunch. This was a team of individuals not willing and quite possibly not able to take the initiative. Maybe they had never been empowered to do so. My conversations with them lacked energy—their voices were monotone, almost robotic. Where was the excitement, the drive to do and be the best that's so indicative of world-class teams? (Golden Rule #2).

Part of the needs analysis would focus on what members of the team were capable of doing in respect to their current roles.

- Did they have new/different ideas for improvement?
- Did they like the work they were doing?
- Did they like managing people?
- What had they accomplished that needed to be acknowledged?

By learning and assessing their respective capacities, I could better determine their potential for contribution to the growth of the division.

A Nightmare Scenario Emerges

To understand why client turnover was so high, I needed to know how the people within the department treated each other and why. My dad would have liked this approach. He was a third-generation tailor who taught my sister and me, early on, that how you look on the outside—what you wear and how it's worn—tells a lot about the person on the inside, how you think, your biases, judgments, and level of self-awareness.

My first step was to observe how the salespeople interacted with the service folks. Per my dad's guidance, how they thought about the service department, even if only to themselves, would "dress up" or manifest in the way they treated them face-to-face. It didn't take long to notice that the salespeople showed little respect for the service team. In return, the service team harbored nothing but resentment and contempt toward them.

Can you say nightmare? Divisive? Civil war? At each other's throats? Can you say "business as usual?"

For example, when a salesperson got a new client, this would require the completion of a new client form. The common practice was for the salesperson to enter only the name of the client and telephone number on the sheet. The salesperson would then drop the form on the desk of an assigned service person. The salesperson assumed the service person would call the prospective client and get all the information needed for onboarding. Miffed, the service people would make those follow-up calls while upset, which meant what they were feeling inside was showing up on the outside (not the best way to make good impressions with new clients).

When I observed the actual way sales were made, it was not surprising to learn that most of the salespeople bypassed the company's formal sales process and did things in ways that were most convenient for them. They earned commission when a client was onboarded, and the service people did 90% of the work (whereas about 25% should have been the salesperson's responsibility).

There was no collaboration between sales and service, thus no opportunity to appreciate the role each team played in client care and successful client onboarding, and certainly no gratitude demonstrated between the two vital functions. No small group dynamic existed to resolve issues and problem solve, either. Salespeople simply received their commissions even though the service people did most of the work.

I needed to get these teams in a room together to create one small group dynamic to ease the feelings of rivalry and the willingness to sabotage. Both sales and service needed to realize they were on the same team, going after the same objectives, and that they needed to collaborate for the division to be as successful as possible (Golden Rule #3):

- The salespeople needed to realize that without the service people, 70% of all orders would not be processed to the standard necessary for them to receive their commissions.

- The service people needed to understand that without sales there was no money, no salaries, no jobs, no company.

Intimidation, Bullying, and Videotape

Approximately three months into the project, the chief financial officer asked to meet with me at company headquarters. He wanted to better understand how, what, and why I was doing what I was doing, and to discuss an operating budget for the fiscal year. I was a bit perplexed that the CFO would want to meet with someone at least three levels below him rather than his direct reports. I had come to learn that this was an organization whose culture was wrapped up in "that's not how we do things here" and "we've never done it that way before." His invitation seemed to buck the company line.

The night before my meeting with the CFO, I flew into the city where the company was headquartered. I was thinking it's a finance meeting because why else would the CFO care about what I am going to do to make his numbers?

(My experience is that CFOs only want to know the results of actions taken by "change agents" like me—and then primarily only the money and numbers related to success. Most of the time, they truly don't care about why we do what we do.)

The next morning, I arrived at the company's reception area where all visitors were required to check in with security. I was greeted with a kind welcome and asked to wait. About 15 minutes later, Thomas stepped out of the elevator and walked over to greet me. Immediately, he asked me to follow him down an adjoining corridor into a sizable conference room. He never stopped to shake my hand, tell me it was good to see me, or offer a simple, "Good morning."

Corporate culture is typically top down, and he was at the top, so suddenly it made sense why his direct reports were less than enthusiastic when we first met. They were playing a grown-up version of follow the leader!

Thomas steered me into the boardroom. The oblong, wooden table at its center had what looked like 25 seats surrounding it. I didn't do an exact count. In my book, any table that sits more than 12 people is superfluous to a productive meeting, so I figured out right away that if all those chairs got filled, nothing was going to get done, decisions would not be made.

Thomas acted anxious. I wondered if he feared that I might embarrass him in front of the CFO. I noticed that he seemed to be imitating holding a cigarette, as though he was ready to take a drag. This looked just like what my mom used to do when she was smoking.

He needs a smoke before this meeting, I told myself and, sure enough, Thomas excused himself and exited. Five minutes later, he came back, practically exhaling the last drag on his cigarette as he entered the room. It stunk to holy hell with just the two of us in there. I hoped that once more people appeared, the room temperature would increase and the HVAC system would kick in and rid us of the stench.

Five minutes before the start time on the agenda, Thomas and I were still the only people in the room. I noticed a video camera facing a chair positioned at one end of the table.

Hmmm...

Not sure what to expect, butterflies took flight in my stomach, and I was pretty sure Thomas was already thinking about his next smoke. He was doing that imitation smoking thing again, which was really strange. Maybe it was nothing more neurotic than biting fingernails, something I've been guilty of on occasion. Nevertheless, he seemed more worried than me.

A few minutes later, people start drifting into the room. Some 20 minutes after that, the CEO (Thomas's boss) and the CFO appeared. Like they were the Red Sea parting for Moses, people shifted left and right, creating an aisle so the two could walk to the table and take what appeared to be preassigned seats. It all felt a little pompous and arrogant to me, almost premeditated.

Since I was the guest, I remained standing until it was obvious that only one seat remained, the one at the end.

Should I grab it? I wondered. *Was this some bizarre form of corporate musical chairs?*

I couldn't help but think, as division leader, Thomas should have provided some guidance as to what to expect and the proper etiquette for this encounter. *What's coming next? Am I prepared for it?*

I took the last seat and composed myself. That's when I noticed the aforementioned video camera was pointed at me. Now I knew, *I* was to be the star of this movie.

The CEO and CFO appeared like caricatures of themselves. The CEO was wearing a blue suit, red and blue striped tie, and white shirt. His hair was impeccable. Every strand was perfectly placed. The CFO was a robust individual, on the larger side. I couldn't help but think he might have been an athlete in his younger days. I noticed that his hands were huge—his fingers double the girth of mine. I imagined that once we got around to shaking hands, he would squeeze mine hard to get a reaction. His whole demeanor seemed to be about intimidation. I recalled something my father used to say to help keep proper perspective, "The bigger they are the harder they fall."

In preparation for this meeting, I had provided documentation for budget discussions to attendees earlier in the week. Now I had this documentation in front of me, as did the attendees.

The CFO swiveled his head, catching the eyes of everyone around the table. He cleared his throat and began to speak.

"It's like an annual rite of passage," more than one of my peers had told me prior to the meeting. "It's like an initiation into a fraternity. Expect a lot of drama, disconnected criticisms related to your budget, dismissive comments, marginalizing commentary, and outright offensive language."

Great! So, I should expect bullying and demeaning tactics to ensure I remain subordinate. Bring it on!

The CFO gave instructions to the audio-visual tech to turn the video and audio on.

"This session is being recorded and I need everyone to acknowledge their understanding of this with a verbal 'yes,'" he said. I felt like I was sitting in the exit row on an airplane. The only difference was the people in this room didn't care whether you were physically able to open any emergency doors.

The CFO explained how he had heard about all the "great" actions I wanted to implement. He then asked me to explain my budget from start to finish and to speak loudly and clearly enough to be recorded.

Before I jumped in, I asked the CFO if he wanted me to accentuate any parts of the budget or rationalize the numbers more than what I provided in the assumptions. Surprisingly, he responded by simply repeating his original request.

So that's what I did, reading each line item verbatim:

- Sales, blah, blah, blah.
- Total revenue sources, blah, blah, blah.
- Subtotal revenue sources, blah, blah, blah.
- Expense items, blah, blah, blah.

You get the drift. For 90 minutes I continued with the monotonous exercise. It was a drag for me. I couldn't imagine how dull it must be for those in the room or even those who might watch my epic performance later on video. As I spoke, I tried to pay attention to the body language and facial expressions of the others, especially Thomas and the CFO.

Thomas was doing the best imitation chain-smoking I'd ever seen. As for the CFO, well that was another awesome sight! He was getting more and more fidgety and redder in the face, as though he was a human gasket ready to blow. By the time I completed my remarks, he was clearly trying to restrain himself.

When I was done, Thomas asked if I had anything more to share. I told him I wanted to restate my assumptions, so I went through those as well. By then, this all felt like a pointless exercise. I had sent them my budget a week in advance, so I had no idea why they asked me to walk them through it on camera.

Hey, not my party.

The CFO thanked me for the information and then started his line of questioning. His tone was mild-mannered at this juncture, but I could tell he was building up to something, as though he was looking forward to ripping me a "new one." I just didn't know what points from my explanation and spreadsheets could possibly have gotten his nose so out of joint.

Before he got into his "zone," he reminded me that the video had been running the whole time. With that, the feedback, possible reprimand, and berating began. He was like a bull in a China shop with the awareness of a sleepwalker. He yelled at me, questioning my logic and where I got the numbers from.

"Who do you think you are, presenting this budget to me, the CEO, and Thomas?" He asked.

His rant went on for about an hour. I took notes. Most importantly, I tried to write out the questions he spewed, some verbatim. I figured I would provide my answers using some of his own medicine if given the chance.

Once he completed the inquisition, we all took a 30-minute break. It was more than enough time for me to get some water, fresh air, clear my head, and prepare for more of the same.

When the meeting resumed, I remained respectful of the other attendees, waiting for everyone else to sit down before I did.

As expected, the CFO picked up right where he left off. He asked if I thought I could answer all of his questions from earlier in a satisfactory manner. "If you can do that and I approve your answers, we can be done and get moving on for the year," he explained. "If not, you have two more days of going through this bullshit to get it right."

He asked if I learned anything from the first session and, if I did, he wanted to know what I learned.

I glanced at the other attendees. They appeared to be sitting on the edge of their seats waiting with bated breath to hear what came out of my mouth. It was as though they were anticipating the gate to open for the bull in a bullfight.

I looked at the CFO, repeated his question and said, "No, I didn't learn anything from what you said in the previous session." I wish I could have taken a picture of the reactions of everyone in the room, especially the CFO. I even noticed that the CEO's eyes were opened wider than they had been all day.

Maybe he'd finally heard something worthwhile after so many years at the helm!

Thomas took a deeper breath than usual. I'm not sure if it was due to my response, the lack of capacity of his lungs from smoking, or a combination. My division's controller sat there with forehead in hand shaking his head. The CFO pounded his fist on the table and yelled at me. He couldn't believe I hadn't learned anything.

Looking him in the eye, I said calmly (changing his name here to protect the guilty), "Mike, you were yelling at me the whole time. In fact, you were so loud I couldn't hear a word you were saying. It was as if we were in an echo chamber with bad acoustics and I couldn't decipher the words. So no, I didn't hear most of what you said. The result is I didn't learn a thing."

He stood erect, pushed his chair aside, and stormed out of the room. I thought he was going to explode or, at a minimum, pop the top button off his shirt. Either that or he might come back and fire me on the spot.

He returned about five minutes later. He calmly told me I would get a copy of the video from that day. He said I should take it to my hotel room and be prepared to answer all of the questions I didn't hear him ask of me. He walked out and the CEO followed. On the way out, the controller offered his business card and said I could call if I needed anything. Thomas looked at me like a disappointed father, as though I had shamed him. I had nothing to offer to console him. He did give me some insight, though—finally!—for the next day's session. He said the same thing would happen unless I was prepared to respond differently. I told him I would be prepared.

I received the video a short time later and went back to my hotel room. Sitting at the small desk in my room, I played the video. The first time I watched it like I would a movie. (I must admit, it was an epic performance!) The second time through, I tried to notice nuances about the questions, the order, the flow. Was there something there that would give me insights as to what the CFO was really looking for? What did he want my response to be to this charade? Should I change my numbers to lower the budget? Should I lower the hiring target, raise the revenue numbers? Whatever he wanted was not obvious.

I watched the video a few more times feature film style to see if I could pick up on some clues and cues. I decided to go question by question to ensure I had answers for him. If I had the tape, he certainly would have a copy as well. I was sure he was scrutinizing his performance and mine, trying to find some more ammunition to add to this arduous exercise.

The next morning, as we began to gather for the meeting, I was hoping for some kind of dialogue so I could learn their processes, priorities, the financial ratios they wanted me to focus on, the profit margin targets, etc. I was prepared to raise revenue objectives, lower hiring numbers—you name it. I was also prepared for more of the CFO's irate nonsense.

Just like yesterday, he asked the tech person to start the camera and away we went. Mike repeated his question. "Did you learn anything from yesterday's session?"

I said, "I don't know. I reviewed the tape several times and what I have prepared for today will hopefully tell us if I learned anything."

Mike directed me to answer one of the questions from yesterday. I skimmed my list of questions from the video and the corresponding answers, rattling off a series of changes I interpreted had to be made based on what I heard in the video.

With a smug smile on his face, Mike thanked me for my effort. "You did learn something after all," he said.

Here it comes, I thought. I knew he had been waiting to pounce on something. So I buckled up, strapped in, and held on tight.

He then ran through a long list of items, yelling again, and this was a new list, different from what was in the video.

Then I got it! This was his way to influence the budget he wanted for whatever reason. It wouldn't have mattered if I said exactly what he wanted me to say. He would spin his responses so he would always appear to come out right. He was taking the old, "if I want *your* opinion, I'll give it to you" approach.

This was a pivotal moment, one where I got to choose the path for moving forward.

As the CFO continued his rant, in my periphery I saw that Thomas and the CEO seemed at ease, calm, poised even. Then it hit me. All of the drama was choreographed. This team had probably done the same dance so many times before that it had become second nature, a habit.

My peer had been right when he warned me this meeting was an initiation of sorts. Indeed, it was. Message received!

...Quick to the Truth to Find a Solution

At the end of the second day, I was given the new tape to review and prepare for day number three.

I kept asking myself, "Do I acquiesce, surrender, submit?" I was brought in to be a change agent and get the business back on track. I had experience doing this sort of thing and achieving desired results.

My answer suddenly became clear. This was just like the senior and junior executives I dealt with at another company. They had been so worried about the numbers they never saw that the answer was in the people.

My gut and my brain told me to stick with my convictions and not surrender. I'd been there about three months, so I had gotten to know the people well. I might not have known the business well enough to make comments on the numbers—and no one ever sat down with me, least of all Thomas, to explain the key performance indicators—but I did know *the people*.

Go with what you know, my inner voice advised.

I reviewed the tape several times that second night. From the looks of things, the CFO, CEO, and Thomas appeared content with the day's results. They probably left the meeting believing I would return tomorrow and agree to all of Mike's requests.

Instead of answering the CFO's questions with depth, I spent my time writing a closing argument focused on why they needed to let me do what I wanted to do the way I wanted to do it.

The next morning, I got to the conference room about 15 minutes early. Thomas walked in and asked me why I was so early. I felt like responding, "Really? Still no good morning? Still no pleasantries like, 'How are you?' or 'Are you prepared for today's meeting?' or 'Are there any last-minute items/ questions I can help you with?'" but I held my tongue. (There's a first time for everything.)

The controller entered, then the tech person, and finally the CEO. Not one of them said "Hello," or "Good Morning," or anything.

The CEO went immediately to his customary seat and started reviewing some documents. The controller sat and pulled out the financials. The tech person avoided all eye contact, and then Mike, the CFO, honored us with his presence. He walked in with a mug filled with coffee. This was new—a new prop he'd been keeping for the third act of his play.

While I was counting on them thinking this would be just another "been there, done that" wrap-up to the three days of meetings, what they didn't yet understand was that this time their play was going to have a different ending—no more same old, same old.

Mike started the conversation by saying he believed today would be the final session of the budget conversation. "We will walk out of this conference room with a budget we can all agree to for this fiscal year," he declared. He asked the CEO if he had any questions, then Thomas, then the controller. They all shook their heads side-to-side and said, "No."

Mike then scolded me for being disrespectful in the first two sessions. He reprimanded me for not being clearer and more concise with my numbers. "There's too much wiggle room in your budget," he said, sharing that the last two days were important for him to teach me a lesson on refining budgets, focusing on what matters, and letting me know that I *do* answer to the people in the room.

Finally, he was being unambiguous. I truly wished he had shared the purpose and intention for the meeting from the very beginning (Golden Rule #3).

Not once did he refer to what my goal was in this budget effort. Not once did he acknowledge anything about my thought process or even try to understand where I was coming from. In *not* doing so, he had stepped right into my plan. It was almost time for me to be the greatest version of a change agent I could be if I was going to play a role in getting this division back on track.

I waited for Mike to finish. Once he sat down, Thomas told me it was my turn to present my "modified" budget (thus validating my suspicion this was all rehearsed). I just had to play my part—at least my part as they envisioned it.

I opened my folder and neatly placed the financial documents to my left. I then took a pile of papers containing my notes from the two previous sessions and neatly placed them to my right.

It was then I noticed the CEO seemed distracted. I wondered if he really enjoyed these meetings, thinking how I would love to get his opinion one day, just not today. Thomas was starting to imitate smoking again, and the controller looked at me in awe. He seemed to be thinking, "What is this guy doing?"

I then pulled out my written closing argument. It contained little if any commentary regarding me changing the numbers. Yes, there were some items the CFO made abundantly clear needed to be changed or he would change them. But outside of those few numbers, I didn't change a thing. I gave them a speech similar to what I'd given past clients, citing the need to focus on people rather than numbers or be doomed to fail. I noted that financials don't provide an indication of what's happening right now and can't predict future performance. Financials are lagging indicators. People are indicative of the future. Surround yourself with a world-class team (Golden Rule #2), let them do their jobs (Golden Rule #1), and the results will speak for themselves.

"The budget is a framework for turning around this business," I said. "It's quite possible that we are successful faster, in which case these numbers would impede growth. It's also possible we are not as successful, meaning we will have to recalibrate and adjust. The key here, for me, is what the barriers are to effective communication and whether we have the right people in place to make this happen:

- Do the people like working here?
- Do they like their jobs?
- Are we optimizing on the constraints?
- Do they feel satisfied?
- Do they feel respected?
- Are they contributing?
- Are they being heard?"

I noted that I was more concerned about adjusting the teams than worrying about the numbers.

"My response may not be what you expected," I continued. "I was brought on by Thomas to be a change agent and this is my approach. You didn't engage me to be another bobblehead at the table doing things the way they've always been done. That is the antithesis of change. I am ready to start taking action on this plan. If in six months we're not clearly in a positive trend and headed in the right direction, we'll do it your way or you can cancel the engagement. I'm hopeful that as we move into the future, *you* will teach me a few things about what really matters to you and how you think about this business. I look forward to that day. In the meantime, does anyone have any questions for me? Is there anything I can clarify? If not, I've got a plane to catch and one heck of a project to get started!"

Success—and a Job Now Done

I convened small group dynamic meetings specifically targeting the strained relationship between the salespeople and service people. The goal was for both sides to come together, engage in dialogue, and really begin to understand each other's challenges (Golden Rule #3).

The first phase of this transformative journey lasted about six months. By the end of it, people had settled in and realized that the need to be right in every disagreement created conflict and resentment, with little, if anything, getting resolved (Golden Rule #3).

Actually, the anger and stress increased at first. There was even a point when the customer retention numbers got worse and less was paid out in commissions and bonuses.

About nine months into the first year, however, relationships began to mend and heal. Make no mistake, there was plenty of work to do for some. As expected, we did lose a few employees. The appropriate behavior of collaboration and paying attention to the tension reinforced the change in results. Customer retention for the first time in about three years began to increase.

This particular small group dynamic concluded that the service folks needed to get a portion of the commission, not just the salespeople. Service came up with a percentage and we worked through the details until mutual agreement was achieved in about two months.

By the end of my tenure, three and a half years later:

- Client attrition dropped to 24% from 42% annually, which was in line with the industry standard.

- Employee turnover was down to 19% from 34%, also more in line with the industry standard.

- Revenues, margins, commissions, camaraderie, and sense of contribution were all up.

- The division grew from $400 million to $750 million

in sales, with 3,500 employees nationwide housed in more than 125 branches and satellite offices.

- Sales grew on average approximately 20% to 25% per year.

- Less dollars invested in recruiting due to higher employee retention meant more funds available to invest in employee education and training.

Way back at the beginning, Thomas and I had discussed getting to this point one day—the day called "success"—and what would come next. It was even spelled out in the engagement agreement.

Since we were at that pre-defined juncture in the journey of transformation for his division, I reached out to Thomas's assistant. I asked her if there was a day on Thomas' calendar within the next week or two when Thomas and I could meet.

She asked if this was for an in-person or telephone meeting. "If it's in-person, will you be coming to corporate headquarters or are you expecting Thomas to visit you at your office?"

"This will be in-person," I replied. "I will travel to headquarters."

"Did *you* need anything else?" She asked. "Does Thomas need to prepare anything?"

"No," I said and thanked her for her help.

A couple of weeks later, the day of my meeting with Thomas finally arrived. I had not heard a word from him by phone or email. I entered the building where the infamous three-day budget meeting took place and made my way to his office.

I walked in and he lifted his head. "Friedman, what the f**k are you doing here?"

"What do you mean? The appointment's on the calendar."

"I know we have an appointment," he groused. "But I thought it was by phone."

I shook my head. "I requested an in-person meeting. This was too important a conversation for a phone call."

I reached into my coat and drew a folded piece of paper from the inside breast pocket. Thomas didn't know it yet, but this was my notification that ended our engagement, per the terms of the initial agreement. I handed it to him.

Thomas gave it a quick read. He looked like he was in shock. "I didn't see this coming."

I believed him. I still do. He probably thought I would stick around forever in servitude because that's how most executives think: anyone on the team serves at the leader's discretion and should be comfortable with an open-ended arrangement.

"Why now?" He asked.

"We've been discussing this day for the past three years," I explained. "The day has arrived, and you haven't offered me a position of president in another division, per our deal, so I am ending the engagement."

Seemingly desperate, Thomas asked, "Is there anything I can do? More pay? Stock options?"

While it was nice to feel wanted, I told him that had those kinds of questions been part of our ongoing discussions, we probably wouldn't be at this juncture.

"Thank you for the experience," I said. "I really mean it. And I'm grateful for the offer you just put on the table." *Perhaps, this is a lesson learned for us both*, I thought. *Never assume people will stick around just for the sake of sticking around, and never take anyone or anything for granted.*

I handed him his company property—a laptop and my access key for getting into the building—and gave him my business card should he need to reach out. I also shared that I was available to him and the entire team for four more weeks.

I had seen the work through to completion. As a team, we had gone beyond what anyone thought was possible; we had moved mountains. While the ending could have been different—but not necessarily better—my hunch told me it was time to move on.

Golden Rule #1: "Owners/leaders don't solve problems."

Golden Rule #2: "Surround yourself with people who get excited by thinking/acting like owners."

Golden Rule #3: "Communicate with a high relevance factor."

Contact STUART FRIEDMAN:

stuart@leadersdontsolveproblems.com | (312) 543-0013

---

4 | PENNY WISE AND POUND FOOLISH

I was giving an engagement kickoff presentation at the offices of a new client. Participants included my new client, Mary, seven others—her direct reports, presumably—and me.

This particular presentation was the beginning phase of the engagement with Mary and her team. I made it before meeting one-on-one with the executives involved in the engagement to introduce new terminology, planned phases for the engagement, timelines, metrics, and to set expectations.

As planned, the presentation took three hours. I distributed materials, we had conversations about next steps, and Mary concluded the meeting. I judged it to be a very productive session. Based on the energy level in the room, it appeared everyone else did too.

Fast forward three months and I was speaking at an industry conference. It was an opportunity Mary had helped arrange by submitting my name to conference organizers. I completed my talk on "effective hiring," started exiting the stage, and saw Mary approaching. I was wondering if I would see her and, if so, when. It was a pleasant surprise. She complimented my presentation, then introduced me to a man who was standing next to her. He looked familiar, but I couldn't quite place him.

The man introduced himself as "Jason." He said this was the second time he had observed me and some of the work I do. The first time, he explained, had been during the kickoff presentation I did for Mary and her team. Apparently, Mary had not limited attendees to just her direct reports!

Mary smiled and said she'd leave us to talk, so I thanked her for the introduction. Now that Jason and I were alone, I asked him what was on his mind.

He shared that he wanted to "make a lot of f**king money"—that it was his sole purpose for starting his business. "I make deals, my salespeople make deals, and I get a percentage of their deals," he said, explaining how his business worked. "And I'm the one putting up the money to procure some of the deals. Essentially, I'm the bank, the private equity if you will."

I learned Jason owned an organization that was involved in large dollar transactions related to real estate around the world. He was the originator of most of the company's deals, and he had a network of referral sources that was vast and productive. From what I could tell, this was a highly lucrative enterprise with a great business model. Jason was on a mission to make money, and lots of it. To top things off, his communication style was clear and unambiguous. His focus was laser-like. This was appealing.

Be Careful What You Ask For

Jason explained how he thought he had hired people who wanted to make a lot of money like him. "Based on their interviews alone, I was under the impression they were hunters rather than farmers," he said. "But they just aren't producing like I want them to. They're not hitting their numbers and I'm still doing most of the lead generation."

I suggested the two of us should meet soon to discuss his approach to hiring, so we set up a time.

About two weeks later I was sitting in Jason's office listening to him describe his business, his role, the role of his sales team, and his approach to hiring them:

- Given his stature in the industry, Jason felt his time and effort were only worth spending on deals expected to gross at least $25 million.

- If the expected dollar outcome of a deal was not at least $25 million, he would pass it on to one of his salespeople, figuring such lesser deals were essentially busy work for them.

- Because they were getting paid a salary, he had his sales team handle the administrative details of all company deals—both his and theirs.

- Keeping his salespeople working the deals Jason did not want to handle limited their ability to be proactive about their own deals.

My takeaway from what he shared was that his sales hires seemed very good at taking orders and keeping busy, but that did not necessarily make them good at sales. I suggested he let me observe some of his upcoming interviews.

"I don't understand why sales year-over-year and year-to-date aren't better," he wondered aloud. "Why aren't my salespeople doing more, creating better deals?"

We were about to find out.

Cut to the Chase to Find the Problem...

Over the next few weeks, I sat in on several interviews with prospective hires.

On the surface, the interviews seemed "normal," but Jason was clearly not a trained interviewer. He asked innocuous questions and applicants gave canned answers. He also made inexperienced interviewer errors repeatedly, asking closed-ended questions where a "yes" or "no" answer would suffice.

Experienced interviewers know there is far more to learn about an individual beyond simple "yes" or "no" answers. Understanding why a "yes" or "no" answer gets shared is also critical. Accepting curt "yes" or "no" or simplistic answers at face value does not provide the information necessary to move beyond "let's hire and hope" to make good hiring decisions. Where is the proof or evidence to back up or expand upon what an individual shares?

I did not judge Jason's approach as either good or bad, right or wrong. Rather, his methods simply did not allow him to explore the motivations, desires, and biases of interviewees—all those things Jason *should* want to know to ensure a good hire who was aligned with his way of thinking and working.

Near the end of each interview, he would ask candidates if they had questions. Again, there was really nothing wrong or out of the ordinary with his approach. I just thanked the Lord he didn't ask any inappropriate questions!

After the sessions, Jason and I met for a debrief in his office. He asked me what I had observed.

"I don't think any of these applicants are going to satisfy your desire to hire only people who want to make a lot of money," I replied.

He seemed perplexed. "According to their resumes and their answers, they seem like really good salespeople," he countered.

"You didn't ask any questions that would reveal proof or evidence of their 'successful' histories, and how that might apply to *your* business," I offered. "I'm not doubting their abilities. Maybe they are really good salespeople, but in what environment? In your business, people need to be curious. They need to investigate, ask questions, be autonomous in their daily activities, and not get stuck making decisions good or bad...just like you."

Now, Jason *did* ask candidates what made them think they would be successful. Most said they would do "anything necessary to close a deal" because money was their incentive. He also asked if they would be willing to work nights and weekends. Most replied "Yes, if necessary."

To me, these answers seemed like afterthoughts. None of the candidates volunteered the information. They all had to be asked.

As for any questions they might have, most inquired about benefits, time off, and even specific time off in the future if hired due to vacations already scheduled.

"Given all that, does it sound like earning money—a lot of money—is a priority for any of these people?" I asked Jason. "Think about it. If a deal was pending the day before one of these candidates was scheduled for vacation, do you think that candidate would delay taking vacation like *you* would? Would that candidate be proactive and get the deal done before going, like *you* would? Do you think any of them would be as passionate about *their* business as you are passionate about yours?"

Jason shrugged. He nodded his head. "I suppose not," he said.

"You need to make a shift in your paradigm for hiring salespeople," I advised. "You need to hire only people whose perspectives on priorities and what really matters to them—which in your case is to make a lot of 'effing' money—align with yours" (Golden Rule #2).

The Fine Print

Part two of my engagement was a needs analysis. For two weeks, I observed the salespeople going about their daily activities and listened to their phone calls with current and prospective clients.

I found that most were unable to "ask" for the business. Instead, the salesperson would keep offering information until the other party agreed to a deal. Then, the salesperson would schedule necessary activities to complete the process, which usually took about three to four months. While this seemed reasonable, preparing the paperwork and doing the follow-up necessary should have been a two- to three-month process at most.

I sensed little urgency with any member of the sales team. Why would there be? They got paid the same salary whether a deal closed in two months or four months. Jason did not hold any of them accountable for timing the close. He might complain about how cash flow was behind schedule, but he rarely met with his team to gather information about works-in-progress, timing, etc.

I asked Jason for a copy of the standard sales contract he used when hiring his team. The document contained the usual terms describing salary and commissions and bonuses. Based on sales, year-over-year, and salary plus bonus, each salesperson could earn between $150K to $200K simply by showing up every day and maintaining the status quo.

Then I saw it—the golden nugget I was looking for, the glimmer of an incentive that could light a fire under at least some members of the sales team to go above and beyond. It was buried toward the end of the document. The language was plain and simple: if salespeople bring in deals of their own at or above $10 million in revenue, they earn a 4% commission on balances above $10 million.

Holy smokes! I thought, doing the math. *Now that's an incentive!*

I also learned that Jason brings in about seven to eight of these mega deals each year while the salespeople rarely do.

Hmmm?

Cutting Off Your Nose to Spite Your Face

Then it happened. A salesperson landed a $37 million deal. Once the deal closed, the CFO informed me the funds had been transferred to the company's account. This meant the salesperson could be paid his commission.

The CFO and I went to Jason, excited to deliver the news that one of his salespeople had brought in a huge deal.

"The money's been funded to our company account," the CFO said, almost gleefully. "It's time to cut a check to the salesperson, per the sales contract, for 4% or $1.08 million."

Jason turned beet red. Every muscle in his jaw clenched. I remember thinking, *If he was a machine, smoke would be pouring out of his ears right now.*

With zero ambiguity, he blurted, "I'm not paying a million-dollar commission to a f**king salesperson. No f**king way that's happening. Over my dead body!"

Both the CFO and I were incredulous. I piped in and reminded him that the sales contract stipulated a 4% commission.

"No f**king way that's happening," Jason repeated.

The CFO and I left Jason's office together and we regrouped in the CFO's office.

"This is not right," the CFO said and looked at me. "What should we do?"

I suggested he cut the check and have it ready for signature.

"The bigger issue is what do you do when the salesperson comes to your office looking for the check? What do you say, that Jason said, 'No f**king way'?"

Beyond the salesperson being furious—we weren't talking chump change here—I could envision the following: disengagement, resentment, quitting, and a lawsuit.

Eventually, the salesperson learned the deal officially closed and was funded. Sure enough, he went to the CFO's office and asked when he could expect to be paid. The CFO explained that for such a large check there were a couple of security items that had to take place to transfer the money, which could take up to two weeks.

Two weeks passed and the salesperson followed up by meeting with the CFO and me, inquiring about the check.

"You'll be getting it soon," the CFO said. "Hopefully this week."

From the salesperson's reaction, I could tell he was not taking the delay well. He seemed frustrated and wanted to get paid. He had every reason to expect the payment to be timely. Who could blame him?

...Quick to the Truth to Find a Solution

Following our encounter with the salesperson, the CFO and I went to Jason's office with the check we had prepared to be signed. Again, Jason declared, "There is no way I'm paying a f**king salesperson 1.08 million dollars. He can go f**k himself."

That's when I suggested to Jason that he tell the salesperson that he's "not paying a f**king salesperson" the commission as stipulated in a contract signed by him, the owner. I reminded Jason that for the $1.08 million commission, he had received more than $10 million in profits, a nice return on investment for him essentially doing nothing.

"That's the nature of offering incentives," I explained.

I also outlined for him what might occur if he did not pay:

- Your word and your brand won't be worth anything to the other salespeople and employees.

- No one on the sales team will be motivated to take on such a big deal again. They will most likely say "F**k Jason."

- The salesperson will most likely quit and go to a competitor, where he'll be motivated to kick his former boss's butt (that's you).

- The salesperson will make sure your industry knows what kind of person you are and how you treat people.

- The salesperson has the "smoking gun" in the signed contract and will win a lawsuit or force a settlement for *more* than $1.08 million.

Jason seemed to contemplate his options for about a minute. Finally, he said, "F**k it! Let's pay this asshole."

"Let's pay this a**hole?" I repeated. "You mean the guy who just put millions in your pocket? That's an interesting definition of an a**hole. I think I'd like a whole bunch of these a**holes working for me!"

Minutes later, we summoned the salesperson into Jason's office to receive the check. Instead of personally handing the check to him and expressing gratitude, Jason told the salesperson his check was in the manilla folder on the desk.

"You can get it yourself."

The CFO and I congratulated the salesperson for a job well done. He thanked us and left.

An Expensive Lesson

About two weeks later, the same salesperson asked the CFO and me to join him in Jason's office for a scheduled appointment. I wondered if he had another outrageous deal. And then it hit me. "Nope, there's no deal. He's quitting."

As the three of us entered Jason's office, Jason barely looked up from his monitor.

"What's this meeting about?" He asked.

Without a word, the salesperson put two pieces of paper on Jason's desk.

"You can see for yourself," he said.

The top sheet was a resignation letter. In it, he wrote that he was so upset by the situation that he found another job at Jason's top competitor. The second sheet of paper was essentially a "white paper," a complaint to be filed for harassment in the workplace.

But the salesperson wasn't done. He let Jason know that as soon as he exited the premises, he would be embarking on a second, even larger deal with the same client on behalf of his new employer.

"The client liked how I communicated with them and how I treated them with gratitude, so they want to do more with me in my new role," he said, looking Jason in the eye. "Thank you for the opportunity. It was a one in $1.08 million experience."

Golden Rule #1: "Owners/leaders don't solve problems."

Golden Rule #2: "Surround yourself with people who get excited by thinking/acting like owners."

Golden Rule #3: "Communicate with a high relevance factor."

Contact STUART FRIEDMAN:
stuart@leadersdontsolveproblems.com | (312) 543-0013

5 | WHAT GOES AROUND, COMES AROUND

A few years back, Curtis, the chief operating officer of a company with approximately 1,500 employees in about 10 venues throughout the United States contacted me. Curtis and I ended up meeting three times, plus I engaged in a series of interviews with the owner/CEO, Dina, and the co-owner/CFO, Gary, who were siblings.

I learned that the original owners of the business—the parents of Dina and Gary—founded the company in the 1950s. Their motto was "Don't fix it if it ain't broke." Band-aids for whatever ailed the company were good enough, especially if that meant less cost and keeping more dollars in their pockets. They truly thought only in terms of return on investment. They were not great at thinking about legacy or securing the future. They were simply OK with "doing what they had always done and getting what they always got" because, quite frankly, that usually meant handsome returns.

As the next generation of owners, Dina and Gary were intelligent, confident, and lived in a world that revolved around creating perception as a means of defining oneself. I am sure if they could have done a reality TV show, they would have. They were constantly name-dropping and discussing who they knew rather than communicating with authenticity and sincerity. To them, being in charge meant they needed to convey the impression they knew the business. It was all about optics.

Dina and Gary graduated with MBAs from top-tier business schools. They agreed in their approach to running the business: be progressive by trying to "update" their industry's manufacturing paradigm with new-age concepts while also investing in the business.

- They brought in new computer systems.
- They brought in new manufacturing equipment.
- They trained the executives they hired and promoted at some of the most prestigious "executive-level" seminars, workshops, and programs.

I was grateful for Dina and Gary. They allowed Curtis to reach out and bring me in to create the possibility of a shift in the way the company operated. I was excited for the opportunity because the owners spoke of growth and innovation during our interviews. I sensed they understood I had been an agent for change in my work to date and that's what they wanted me for.

Their questions of me focused on change and what evidence I could provide of my ability to initiate change, implement change, and get results. In all honesty, I did not think I would get the engagement because I made it abundantly clear that for me to have gotten the results I achieved with others, I often had to push the envelope. I knew Curtis understood my perspective and approach. After all, he was the one who brought me in to speak with the owners in the first place. As for Dina and Gary, I understood their need to get to know me and my way of working better.

After two months of interviews, various testing, and surveys, Curtis signed an engagement letter and I was brought in. I was soon contributing and participating in full, happy that Curtis at least—who was technically my "client"— saw the potential in our collaboration.

Approximately one year into my tenure—amidst an influx of new machinery and updated systems—a noticeable shift in company culture was occurring: people were beginning to change the way they approached their work and each other. The vibe was one of upbeat energy, optimism, and excitement to get to the office and solve the next wave of challenges.

Can you say world-class team?

It was as though the organization had awakened from a deep sleep. Top to bottom, most employees were thinking and acting like owners of their respective areas (Golden Rule #2).

One glorious summer day, I arrived at the company's offices. I took my usual stroll past Curtis's office and did a double take. There were moving boxes piled high. Stepping through his open doorway, I was even more amazed by what I saw: his desk was bare and he was wearing jeans and a T-shirt, not his usual suit and tie.

Did he resign? Was he fired?

After a little probing, Curtis shared that he had resigned. There had been no companywide communication, no retirement party…nada, goose-egg.

"What happened?" I asked.

He didn't say much. He just shook his head and thanked me for the work we did together, gave me his official departure date, and then wished me and the team well. That was the last time I saw him on the premises.

Where does this leave me and the team?

Curtis had been hired by the parent ownership team, not Dina and Gary, with whom he rarely saw eye-to-eye.

How long will they tolerate me in a role given to me by Curtis? I wondered. I had been his choice, not their choice, and now he was gone.

Still, the length of time agreed upon in my engagement letter was three years, so I had a bit of security—if you want to call it that—on my side. I knew that Dina and Gary would need to bring in someone from the outside to fill the COO role—probably someone they already knew. I had no illusions of grandeur that *someone* might be me.

Now Entering the Friend Zone

To replace Curtis, the owners decided to bring in a consultant, Lisa. She was a connection of sorts from their prior lives before owning the company. Their decision to bring Lisa onboard was made unilaterally. Neither Dina nor Gary sought input from me or the team I was leading. As owners, that was their right. My only wish would have been for Lisa to meet with the team and me during the decision process.

The owners clearly wanted to maintain a buffer between various functional activities and people in the organization. This included my functional area, Client Partnerships. Under this new arrangement, I reported to Lisa, not Dina or Gary.

True to form, the owners did not share this exciting news with the team. One morning, Lisa simply called a meeting of my team where she announced that we were now all *her* direct reports. Needless to say, I was not getting a warm and fuzzy feeling.

Lisa had a calming voice and a direct communication style. She was efficient with language, sticking to her agenda for the meeting. She was not rude, oppressive, or dismissive—as far as I could tell.

Over the next few months, Lisa and I coexisted. She did not reveal much to me about the goings-on in the organization, including how my team might be impacted. She did not reveal much at all, actually.

I found that Lisa was compassionate yet objective, pragmatic, and stoic. As I would expect, she was clearly representing the owners and "toeing the party line." If I had been asked at the time to do a 360 review for her, I would have given her an "A+" for loyalty to Dina and Gary. I would have also given her an "Exceeds Expectations" for withholding information relevant to running the department. All the possible unknowns were like torture to me. This included how she would measure whether the team was successful.

I couldn't help but wonder how the team felt. I may have entered into my "I've got nothing to lose," modus operandi, but how the team members felt and whether their jobs were safe was a concern.

The Blind Leading the Sighted

I held a team meeting and included Lisa in the invite. She turned down the offer. At the meeting, team members voiced their perspectives. Naturally, all were concerned. However, most expressed a "let's wait and see what happens" mentality, which in my mind meant they were open to creating possibilities in the near-term.

One aspect of my relationship with Lisa that was frustrating and unfulfilling was that she rarely gave feedback on anyone's performance. Numbers are numbers and I could see where we met expectations and where we exceeded expectations. However, there was little to no conversation about the "journey."

To me, it's the journey that really matters. Outcomes are outcomes, but it's the journey—the ability to shift and recalibrate constantly—that creates a world-class environment and team. The journey also creates an environment to ensure open dialogue in future scenarios where collaboration creates brilliant decision making. This is the kind of small group dynamic that ensures results.

Curtis, the former COO, had provided weekly feedback that included insights from the owners. My team and I needed that kind of feedback.

Lisa made it clear to the team that we would no longer have direct contact with the owners unless Dina and Gary initiated it.

Can you say schism? Can you say isolation? Can you say BS?

Our meetings with the owners had always provided insight into clients, challenges, etc. They were productive conversations and we always had action items coming out of them to better the organization and our client relationships.

I shared these concerns with Lisa. My intention was that she might take the cues and continue the previous approach concerning feedback. She did not. It became clear the owners were betting on Lisa to take on the continued success of the Client Partnerships department in isolation. She was the proxy for the owners; we'd just have to trust her and follow her guidance.

Again, this approach was the owner's prerogative and who was I to argue with their success (other than to argue in the name of greater success, of course)?

Nevertheless, I was perplexed. The Client Partnerships team secured and protected over $100 million a year in revenue through its work and contributions, yet the owners perched a consultant on top of it—something that "ain't broke" and needed no fixing. How Lisa would guide us into the future was anyone's guess. She might toe the line of the owners, but did she think and act like they did?

The fact that there was no ambiguity concerning the culture Dina and Gary wanted to create and maintain was a gift. It was easy to prioritize decisions based on my knowledge of what really mattered to them. This helped me to anticipate and be proactive so we could avoid "misses."

At this point, I had been engaged with the company for 18 months. Lisa had offered little to no feedback as of this juncture, and I was hopeful that would continue. To use a sports analogy, she was the perfect sports referee—she was not noticed. She just did her job and let the "players" play. That was us.

Meanwhile, the Client Partnerships team continued its great record of creating an excellent partnering experience for clients. One of our functions was to ensure teams were fully staffed: internally and externally. As an extension of our efforts, our success drove onboarding and adjusting infrastructure to get a cohesive team in place as quickly as possible.

At about nine months into Lisa's tenure as our go-to, I started sensing something else was going on behind closed doors. I was not alone in my suspicions. The rest of the team felt it too. We could not put our fingers on it exactly, but it seemed as though Lisa was running decisions through the owners. Maybe they weren't being so isolationist after all?

Need to Know = Knowing Nothing

Just about the time I intended to talk with Lisa candidly, she called a meeting of the team. She used the meeting to introduce a retained-search recruiter, meaning this person had an exclusive agreement with the company and a set fee to find qualified candidates.

Was she recruiting for the company? The clients? Both?

The answer was important. As part of our services to clients, the Client Partnerships team was responsible for management hires and directors. Our team had a talented and experienced individual in the role who had been successful procuring right-fit individuals and putting together world-class teams for clients and internally.

The retained-search individual's name was Mardi. She was introduced as a "support effort" to ensure we could keep up with the growth strategy of the company and the increased volume of objectives. I asked Lisa and Mardi in front of the team if we could see that growth strategy and the increased objectives for new clients, current clients, and the organization.

"That information is available on a need-to-know basis only," Lisa replied.

"A need-to-know basis?" I asked, incredulous. "How do we continue our stellar performance and guarantee the margins on our work and the client's work on a need-to-know basis?"

Instinctively, I could see how this would shift our planning approach from being proactive to being reactive, and how our costs would increase two to three times current costs. To me it felt like the organization was being put in the hands of recruiting terrorists.

"Not knowing means we'll be operating at a disadvantage when collaborating with clients and supporting their planning efforts," I noted.

"The owners feel being a reactive organization garners more value," Mardi explained.

So there it was. We were going from a reliable, dependable organization focused on preventing mishaps to one that extinguished mishaps. We were becoming a "go to" organization that solved problems in the moment and excelled at "crisis management," which, I suppose, did have more sex appeal to clients.

Give them what they want, not what they need.

Mardi described how the owners wanted to shift their brand and strategy. I soon realized this new strategy aligned perfectly with Dina and Gary's way of being: create the perception of crisis, solve the crisis, and become the heroes. Being the hero in their minds probably meant they could charge higher fees.

Again, there was nothing wrong with that, and nothing for me to resent. They were the owners, after all. My only frustration was that the increase in effort, energy expended, and costs to be reactive might actually reduce the intended margins in the long run...and this definitely had not been the approach to date for this company.

Lisa announced that she had been given responsibility for the Client Partnerships department. In this role, she had the authority to do as she saw fit to ensure the owners' desires were achieved. Thus, she felt hiring a recruiter like Mardi would up our game for the increase in business activity everyone was expecting.

Naturally, I had some questions for Lisa:

- When was she going to share *all* of the information about changes in strategy?

- Why wasn't the team included in conversations about going forward?

- Did she really need to hire Mardi before giving the team a chance under this new strategy?

My main concern was the team was being marginalized as support staff for Lisa and Mardi. Here was a team of talented individuals, proven performers, passionate workers, and they were being pushed aside. Perhaps this was a way for Lisa and Mardi to indemnify themselves from any messes created by their decisions. They could take action and if there was a screw-up, they could pass blame on to the team—the familiar "goat" (and I don't mean greatest of all time).

At the time, most team members were not in positions to look for jobs elsewhere. Their livelihoods supported families, homes, college tuition, and more. They also tended to be open to taking on new challenges, which in this case they did. They resolved to maintain their own levels of success while also working with Lisa as the new "go-to" and Mardi, her hired gun. Of course, they were not naïve. They knew they would be operating on a need-to-know basis with respect to strategic planning and desired outcomes—and apparently, they had no need to know. They also knew they would not be able to win for losing because they felt any successes they achieved would be "spun" to Mardi and Lisa's advantage.

As for me, I spent about a week contemplating the situation. I wondered about the end game. The hiring of Lisa, who was a friend to the owners, and the hiring of Mardi, who was a friend of Lisa's, would increase expenses so much that my fees plus much of my team's salaries would just be too much for the organization to bear. The writing was on the wall. I/we would be removed at the first opportunity.

I then began to wonder how Lisa and Mardi would do "the dirty deed."

The good news for the owners—which they did not know at the time—was that it did not matter to me as an individual. I was not going to spend my great change-agent energy on such nonsense. I had other clients and corporate partners. I would deliver and depart, no matter the method Lisa and Mardi chose, knowing that Client Partnerships team members served above and beyond as the best versions of themselves.

A "Need-to-Figure-Out-What-To-Know" Basis

A few weeks into Lisa and Mardi's co-tenure, I learned of a client who was looking to hire a new COO. I was the lead on the project due to the senior nature of the position. I consulted with the client to gain clarity on the particulars of the role and the new strategy that would result from the hire. The original recruiter of the team, the client, and I had discussions about the "right-fit" individual.

In collaboration with Mardi, the process was designed to unfold as follows:

- The recruiter searched for candidates and the Client Partnerships team would screen those candidates for viability in respect to management skills/style, communication skills/style, etc.

- The team would determine which candidates continued through the process to be scrutinized by professionals in the client organization to determine if they had the depth of experience, etc.

- I was the final interview in the process. I would collect the information from the prior interviews, assess gaps in information related to each candidate, and seek to fill those gaps. In addition, typically by this time, HR would share information regarding benefits, but not salary.

- During my conversations with candidates, I would let them know the predetermined salary range and bonus structure for the position. I would further explain how the final, actual number was discretionary. It would be determined based on the interviews and what the hiring executive for the client deemed appropriate.

For this particular COO position, there was little if any formal discussion about compensation between Lisa or Mardi and me, and definitely not with the owners.

Historically, compensation had always been determined by the client and the candidate's prospective direct boss. In this scenario, the team's collective opinion about whether or not to hire the candidate was not given consideration by Lisa or Mardi. To me, it seemed as though they had deemed the team unnecessary, irrelevant. Our function, it turned out, was to act as schedulers for the interviewing process.

I hadn't realized that key point. Apparently, I was a little slow on the uptake. *Ugh!*

Since we were on a need-to-know basis, and we hadn't been told anything to change the way we did our jobs, we presumed our roles were necessary. So we continued the usual process: interview, take notes, write them up, deliver to the hiring executive. What we did not know, as of the hiring of Mardi, was that she was circumventing our established, successful approach. Lisa gave Mardi carte blanche to do as she pleased and did not find it necessary to share this detail with us—and neither did Mardi.

I could only presume Mardi was frustrated and/or annoyed that we were trying to engage her in follow-up conversations after interviewing candidates. It was obvious. One day Mardi called an "emergency" meeting with the team. She started the meeting by yelling at us.

"Why are you sending me your interview summaries?" She asked. "I do not care what you think or have to say about the candidates."

"We weren't asked to change our approach or to do anything differently," I explained. "As far as we understood, it was business as usual until we were told otherwise. This is the first I've heard that our participation, other than scheduling, wasn't necessary and to cease our efforts."

Mardi stormed out of the room.

Minutes later, Lisa walked in and demanded to know why Mardi left the room in a rage. Truthfully, I said "I don't know." I shared what happened, how Mardi appeared to be upset with our contributions, and how we were never instructed *not* to participate in the actual hiring process with this COO position.

Mardi then appeared outside the conference room door. Lisa immediately exited and they went off together. I was not privy to any of their conversations, so I can only guess that what Mardi shared with Lisa was not the same as what I shared with Lisa.

It was then that I realized I was essentially operating under a "need-to-figure-out-what-to-know" basis. Of course, what I didn't know then was that filling this COO position was more sensitive than I or any of my team had been told. Our need-to-know in this case was determined by Lisa and Mardi (and perhaps the owners) to be a "don't-need-to-know" basis.

Cut to the Chase to Find the Problem...

After this exchange, our interview notes were no longer requested or required. To prove we were working, I ensured that the team continued to document conversations and activities surrounding recruits, the process, behaviors of other interviewers, etc. Unfortunately, we were now spending more time in the act of CYA (covering your ass), or should I say COA (covering our asses) then in a productive expenditure of energy determining "right fit" to support building a world-class team for this client.

My experience during an interview with one COO candidate was particularly frustrating. Getting in-depth answers was a challenge; I found the candidate less than forthcoming on many inquiries. I could not get specific details about work scenarios, situations relevant to circumstances in past positions, or anything else that could provide insight into this individual's past behavior or performance. I would ask questions a second or third time in a different way, hoping the candidate would share greater insight. I asked open-ended questions, focused on points in his resume, but this individual seemed determined to remain "buttoned-up" about his past.

Our 30-minute conversation should have been at least 60 minutes, and I was getting an inkling that he was hiding something. Something just wasn't adding up. Somehow, I just "knew." He also didn't have many questions for me, other than about benefits, pay, etc.

In my notes for this candidate, I recommended he *not* be moved forward in the process. I met with the Client Partnership team and we discussed him. They were of the same opinion.

Something about the interview did not sit right with me, so I continued to ponder the conversation. The candidate had already spoken with Mardi, so maybe he did not feel obligated to answer my questions fully. Maybe he thought talking to me was just a formality, just going through the motions. Maybe he thought, *I already answered these questions. These people need to get their acts together!* Or maybe he was hiding something.

I decided not to waste good problem-solving energy on what-ifs and maybes. Mardi was not providing her perspective or insights, so I only had his resume and my observations to make a determination. I did not feel he was a "right-fit" candidate...case closed.

Backing the Wrong Horse

Three weeks passed. During this time, the Client Partnership team went on scheduling mode for additional candidates. We cataloged our notes, documented what we did, and so on. Then, I received an awkward voicemail message from Lisa. She asked me to call her as soon as possible. The tone of her voice told me something had happened.

I was in a meeting with a client when Lisa called, so I was only able to return it about two hours later. When she picked up, I could tell I was on speakerphone, and I had no idea who might be listening in. I became hypersensitive to what I said and how I said it, listening for sounds from her end of the call.

She started by asking me how the meeting went with the client. I shared that all was good. She continued on, proclaiming that my services were no longer required.

"Your last day is today," she said.

"Did the company burn down or go bankrupt?" I asked.

There was silence, then I heard whispering.

"The company did not burn down, nor did it go bankrupt," she assured me. She said I lied to a recent candidate for the COO position—the one who, in my mind, had been so frustrating, who seemed to be hiding something.

"How exactly did I lie?" I asked.

"You told the candidate he would get an income of $250,000," she explained. "That's not true, and that puts the owners in an awkward spot."

"What about an investigation? What about seeking the truth?" I asked. "Why not put the candidate and me in a room together and sort this out?"

On the other hand, I thought to myself, *why let a few details ruin a good story?*

Lisa explained how this candidate had been specifically sourced by Mardi—the recruiter getting paid a retainer fee *and* a commission for candidates she sources and hires. Then it dawned on me. All recently hired individuals had been sourced by Mardi. *Cha-ching!* Now I knew why she did not want our contributions.

"My work has been stellar getting results for our clients and for this company. My ethics have never been questioned," I stated. "Now, all of a sudden you find me guilty of a crime. What about due process?"

There was silence on the phone, so I said the only thing I could.

"I wish you all the best."

…Quick to the Truth to Find a Solution

As I hung up, you can imagine what raced through my mind. I was concerned for my reputation, for the team, and about who would coach, mentor, and protect them going forward. I also found some solace in the old adage, "What goes around, comes around." (I'm a firm believer.)

Lisa took the word of a candidate when the only two people in the room were him and me. This was a classic "he said-he said" situation with the favored individual's word—the COO applicant in this case—holding value. Apparently, this was the "dirty deed" opportunity Lisa had been waiting for.

As I am fond of saying, "It is what it is."

Do you want to know what came around? Are you sitting on the edge of your seat? How did Lisa and Mardi contribute to improving the already world-class team in place at the company?

As it turned out, the favored COO candidate was hired despite my recommendation and the recommendations of the team *not* to hire him. As previously mentioned, my engagement came to a screeching halt. Relieved of my role, I moved on to the next client and had no communication with the company for about two years.

Then, quite unexpectedly, I received a call from Dina and Gary's corporate attorney. Apparently, all had not gone well with that particular COO hire. Certain "situations" had come to light.

"Stuart, I read your notes regarding this candidate," the attorney shared. "You were quite clear in your recommendation not to move forward with him. In fact, you wrote, 'do not hire.'"

"That's what I recall," I said.

"As you were accurate with all the other candidates, I don't know why we hired this individual," the attorney continued. "Of course, that doesn't really matter now. The damage has been done."

"What damage is that?" I asked.

The attorney explained how the COO had embezzled funds from the company to the tune of a couple hundred thousand dollars.

"I'm sorry to hear that," I said, and I was genuinely sorry, though I must admit to feeling a bit vindicated. "But why call me?"

"The owners are pressing charges," the attorney advised. "In their due diligence, they are reaching out to all people with whom the COO had contact prior to his hiring. That includes you. We are scheduling depositions in anticipation of a court case. Would you be willing to be deposed?"

There it was. I had something of potential value to Dina and Gary, so now I was suddenly back in their need-to-know graces.

"If they really need me to help build a case, I will have to reach out to my lawyer for legal counsel and advice," I informed the attorney. "If you can get by without me that would be great. I'm really sorry to hear about this situation. This shouldn't happen to anyone. Hopefully, from this debacle will come change to better protect the organization going forward."

Then I wished the attorney all the best.

Golden Rule #1: "Owners/leaders don't solve problems."

Golden Rule #2: "Surround yourself with people who get excited by thinking/acting like owners."

Golden Rule #3: "Communicate with a high relevance factor."

Contact STUART FRIEDMAN:

stuart@leadersdontsolveproblems.com | (312) 543-0013

---

6 | DO YOUR TEAM MEMBERS PLAY BIG ENOUGH?

A colleague once referred me to the owner of a large retailer. She said I should reach out to the owner, who was expecting my call. I asked, "What's on the owner's mind?"

"During the past two meetings of a group of CEOs I get together with monthly, this owner has seemed less than excited about the sales performance of his organization," my colleague explained. "He feels like he's doing all the business development and generating all the activity, while all his salespeople do is call on the same existing clients or prospects over and over. They rarely make calls for new business or get out of the office to meet new prospects. In fact, no one on the sales team seems as excited about growing the business as he does. They're okay with 'good enough' instead of going the extra mile." (Golden Rule #2)

I asked my colleague if all the salespeople reported to the owner—they did—and I thanked her for the intel as we parted ways.

A First Impression to Remember

I reached out to the business owner the next day by phone. My call was answered by a company representative named Carol. She asked me how she could be of service in a way that was both pleasant and sincere—as though she genuinely wanted to help. She made a great first impression. (I remember thinking, *She should be named the company's 'Chief First Impression Officer' or CFIO!'*)

With such an amazing first impression, what might my experience of the rest of the organization be like? Would it be more of the same, something even better, or would it be a letdown?

I gave Carol my name and mentioned that the owner was expecting my call. She asked me to hold, and I had to endure the worst elevator music ever for what felt like minutes. Carol got back on the phone, apologized for the wait (which was in reality probably only about 15 seconds), and told me she was connecting me.

Once on the line with the owner, I introduced myself and shared that I was calling to follow up on my colleague's referral. The owner, Frederick, acknowledged that my colleague was one of the few people he trusts.

"I don't usually reach out for help," he told me in a tone that sounded a little arrogant, bordering on pompous. "All the consultants I've ever met were only worth a 15-minute conversation...max."

I asked Frederick to give me some insight, then, as to why he reached out at the CEO meetings. He repeated everything my colleague had told me, point-by-point.

When he finished outlining the issue, I said to him, "Since you took 20 minutes to tell me your story, I must have passed your qualifier for the average consultant. How about you give me 15 minutes in person to see if I'm worth the conversation?"

Frederick was silent for about five seconds, then said he would be willing to meet with me for *less* than 15 minutes. He asked me to have Carol set up the date and time, and then hung up. Yes, he simply hung up.

I called back and Carol answered. I shared what happened and she started to chuckle. She said that was Frederick's way of testing people to see if they would call back. I asked if having to answer these somewhat wasteful calls was disturbing or upsetting to her.

"It's my job to ensure that all callers, regardless of their reasons for calling, have a good experience," she said. *Wow!* There was nothing mediocre about Carol's perspective. How fortunate Frederick was to have her in the role of CFIO.

An Underutilized Asset

Two weeks later, the date to meet Frederick arrived. While I was interested in meeting him in person, of course, I was actually more intrigued with whether Carol would make as good a first impression in person as she did on the phone.

I arrived for the meeting about 15 minutes early. I wanted to observe the environment, the culture of the business firsthand, especially the CFIO. This would provide me with important insight about how Frederick ran his business. I also wanted to be well prepared for what I expected to be a less than warm welcome from him, so that we could have an incredibly productive and impactful *less than 15-minute* conversation.

I walked into the lobby. There at the front desk was Carol. She was on a call. She smiled and raised her index finger to indicate I should wait. She hung up within seconds and welcomed me by name. "I've been expecting you," she said and suggested I take a seat in the lobby.

I sat down and tuned in to the environment, noting the people walking through the lobby, passing Carol's desk, etc.

Then I heard it! Carol—the CFIO—answered a call with her sincere, "How can I be of service?" greeting. From what I could hear, she was helping someone with product selection, asking pertinent questions so she could connect the caller with the appropriate person in-house.

Soon, I heard Carol say, "You're welcome, let me connect you." Then another call came in. Carol answered again, this time quickly shifting into "sales" mode. A pause told me she was listening to the caller's needs. I heard her counsel the caller on whether the product he or she was looking to buy might be more expensive than what was needed. "We have another model," she said. "It's a lower investment and I believe just as good. It's from a different manufacturer. We carry the product and can ship it to you today."

I listened as Carol collected the caller's billing and shipping information, repeating the information to ensure its accuracy. She thanked the caller for the business and provided her name, noting if the product did not arrive on the date promised, the person should contact her directly.

That was good for another *Wow! Clearly, the CFIO cares!*

I listened in on about three or four more calls, each similar in nature. After approximately 15 minutes, Frederick emerged from behind a closed door off the lobby. He looked at Carol and asked who the gentleman sitting in the waiting area was.

"The gentleman is Stuart Friedman," she said. "He is the consultant you asked me to schedule a 15-minute in-person conversation with."

"Oh, yeah, right," he replied. He looked at me, gestured, and asked me to follow him into his office.

We walked in silence down a short hallway. As I entered his office, I glanced at my watch, noting the time. He had promised me *less than* 15 minutes, so I wanted to know when I was at the 13-minute mark. At that point, I would make a proposal and either get a "yes" to an engagement or some other outcome.

Cut to the Chase to Find the Problem...

I waited for Frederick to sit in the oversized leather chair behind his desk. He did not reach out to shake my hand or ask me to sit. He did nothing. He just looked at me.

"Friedman, I know you've been here for about 15 minutes already," he announced. "What did you learn?"

Of course, with his words I was thinking he and I shared the same desire to cut to the chase.

"Before I share anything, please take out your checkbook. This consulting session is not complimentary," I informed him. "If you want to hear what I have to say, you will need to write out a check payable to 'Stuart Friedman.' Once I see that you've done this, I will give you all the information you want."

He chuckled and said, "I don't pay you until you provide a service."

I assured him our conversation would be less than 15 minutes as he requested. (I checked my watch. I had 12 minutes left.)

He continued to bark but pulled out his checkbook anyway, grumbling how highly irregular this was. I shared that the circumstances were mutual, though I had been called a provocateur before.

Frederick asked the amount, and I told him. He wrote out a check and handed it to me.

Checking my time, I told Frederick I now had 10 minutes to ensure I was not classified as one of his "usual consultants not worth even a 15-minute conversation." I gave him my thoughts:

- You need to give Carol the title of CFIO, making her your company's Chief First Impression Officer.

- With this new title, she needs to be paid way more than what you're paying her now. In fact, she should be paid similar to members of the sales team.

- Carol is doing many of your salespeople's jobs. They are getting commissions due to her smarts, savvy, and care for the company.

- While Carol was answering phones, taking orders, and making sales, I observed many salespeople walk past her desk, seemingly without intention, care, or work to do.

- Not knowing your compensation plans, I can't comment on whether you are enabling your salespeople by not holding them accountable. From what I could see, they clearly do not think or act like you, but Carol sure does. The two of you are in constant action, getting stuff done. I did not get that impression with any of the salespeople.

His reply?

"I'm not paying a f***ing receptionist a salesperson's salary plus bonus and commission. She's a receptionist."

"My impression is that Carol is essentially the glue that makes this place run as well as it does," I told Fredrick. "While I was in the lobby she took sales calls, directing customers to the appropriate people in your organization to ensure the salesperson was credited. She ensured people were happy with the organization's operations and customer experience. She treated every caller with dignity and respect. Not once did I hear her complain about having to do someone else's job." (Golden Rule #2)

Frederick just shook his head.

"My guess is that because of her, your salespeople have lost their drive to get off their rear-ends and make calls or get out of the office to visit existing or prospective customers. She makes it easy for *all* of you…so that is why you should pay her a salesperson's salary plus commission and bonus. Without her, you would need to hire hungry salespeople and you would be complaining about the results, which you said you are not at this point in time."

Frederick was quick to respond. "Friedman, thank you for your interesting perspective of the world. I paid you. You may leave."

I thanked him for his consideration and generosity, noting to him that our conversation ended in 13 minutes. Apparently, I had been worth at least a 13-minute conversation.

… Quick to the Truth to Find a Solution

Frederick and I shook hands and I walked out to the lobby.

There, I approached Carol. I told her it was nice to meet in person and thanked her for allowing me to get comfortable in anticipation of the meeting with Frederick. She didn't ask for my insight, but I shared it with her anyway (as all good consultants do). I told her I thought she was playing "small"— much smaller than what she was capable of.

"Based on my observations, you should be in sales full time," I said. "You're a natural. You'd be a top salesperson."

"No one ever notices my efforts," she told me. "No one ever thanks me for what I do."

I suggested she find the gumption to ask for a promotion to sales—all the while continuing to be a kind, respectful listener, of course.

Carol thanked me and we shook hands before I departed.

About three months later, I received a phone call from Carol. She asked if I remembered her. I said I did, "You're the CFIO!"

She told me what she did after my visit:

- She took to heart the notion of no longer playing small and kept track of her activities for about six weeks.

- She documented the number of calls, the dollars of sales she closed herself, and the dollars of sales she ensured got to the appropriate salesperson.

- She then took that data and presented it to Frederick, along with a request for a promotion to sales.

She explained that Frederick tried to intimidate and bully her out of going through with her request. "He told me, 'Your salary won't be guaranteed,'" she said. "'You might even make less than you do now because you'd be on commissions, which aren't guaranteed.'"

Once Frederick finished trying to talk her out of moving to sales, she simply told him, "If you don't make me a salesperson, I will continue doing my job here as I always have until I find a sales job elsewhere that I think will satisfy my abilities."

Ultimately, Frederick caved—but with one caveat: Carol still needed to sit at the front desk.

"I told him, 'Great, that's what I prefer anyway!'" she told me.

Carol shared that she was the top producer in her first month—with sales orders in the queue for months two and three—and that she was well on her way to becoming the company's most consistent producer.

"Are you proud of yourself?" I asked.

She said she was, thanking me in her gracious way for my help.

"I didn't do anything," I said. "You were already being the best version of yourself every day, getting next level results. All you needed was a little nudge of support. *You* did the hard part. *You* found the certainty and self-worth to take on a new role with passion and to make stuff happen."

Golden Rule #1: "Owners/leaders don't solve problems."

Golden Rule #2: "Surround yourself with people who get excited by thinking/acting like owners."

Golden Rule #3: "Communicate with a high relevance factor."

Contact STUART FRIEDMAN:
stuart@leadersdontsolveproblems.com | (312) 543-0013

7 | AFTERWORD: THE CHOICE IS YOURS

If you've taken anything from these pages (or screens if you are viewing this on an e-reader), then you know that passing judgment, shaming you, telling you you're wrong, etc., was never my intention. You simply are the type of owner and leader you are. Period. Embrace it. The results you've achieved and the results you will enjoy going forward have and will speak for themselves.

Success is not luck. It is the result of hard work, vision, staying your course, honoring your dreams, and driving to achieve where others might not. There is no correct way to get to the destination—no silver bullet or magic pill. There is only you and the world-class team you surround yourself with.

I'm only here to help you shift your paradigm if you want to so you can...

- Get your executives, managers, and key members of your team to think and act like owners.

- Increase revenue momentum.

- Move the "mountain" that you have envisioned.

- Hire the right people to ensure your legacy thrives in the way you deserve and desire.

As to whether you shift or not, the choice is YOURS!

There are at least three possible outcomes for you from reading this book.

1. "Yawn. Next please." (I'm sorry to have wasted your time. We should talk. Please call me at (312) 543-0013 and/or email me at stuart@leadersdontsolveproblems.com).

2. "Interesting, but I'm going to keep doing what I've been doing. It's worked so far." (Good for you. We should still talk. Please call me at (312) 543-0013 and/or email me at stuart@leadersdontsolveproblems.com).

3. "Damn, those are some great points, some golden nuggets. I need to hear more." (I couldn't have said it better. Let's talk. Please call me at (312) 543-0013 and/or email me at stuart@leadersdontsolveproblems.com).

For the above change in thinking to occur, you only need consider living by three golden rules:

Golden Rule #1: "Owners/leaders don't solve problems."

Golden Rule #2: "Surround yourself with people who get excited by thinking/acting like owners."

Golden Rule #3: "Communicate with a high relevance factor."

Leading by these golden rules is not easy; change never is.

There *is* a fourth golden rule:

Golden Rule #4: "You can be right, or you can be in relationship."

Being right means you're stuck always trying to prove you're the smartest, have the best ideas, or that your way is the only way. You need to win at any cost. You tend to lead with, "If I want your opinion, I'll give it to you."

We've seen several examples in this book of leaders who chose to be right:

- Frederick decided that no consultants were worth more than 15 minutes, so he missed an opportunity to collaborate to achieve greater success for his company. Fortunately, a brief encounter with Carol revealed that she was open to possibility and she saw she could play a bigger game.

- Jason said there was no way he'd pay a "f**king salesperson" a million-dollar commission. His need to be right resulted in that salesperson taking the client and millions more in profits elsewhere.

- As proxies for Dina and Gary, Lisa and Mardi hired a COO candidate that my team and I recommended *not* be hired. As a result of Lisa and Mardi's need to be right, the COO went on to embezzle $200,000.

Being in relationship means you choose to be present: you listen, you realize you don't have all the answers, and you seek the input of others. You don't get into debates about whether someone or something is right or wrong or good or bad. You're willing to modify your approach and collaborate with others. You allow members of your world-class team to solve the problems that you don't solve. You let them do their jobs so you can do yours.

We've seen examples in this book of what happens when leaders *choose to be in relationship,* even if reluctantly:

- Thomas, the president of a company division, ultimately worked with me for three years to achieve and sustain profitability. He chose to be in relationship even though Mike, the CFO, started the engagement by berating me for three days.

- It may have taken a baby to silence their profanity, but CEO Pat and his team ultimately chose successful collaboration over continued cursing and dysfunction to achieve greater results than they thought possible.

- "People are not made of numbers, they create the numbers" convinced *the* boss of one company that an overseas project could get back on track, leading to numerous other successful projects and, of course, achieving profitability objectives.

As already established, you don't need to change or fix anything about yourself or the way you lead. You can, however, choose to be right or be in relationship. It *is* a choice, and the choice is YOURS!

To every owner or leader who would rather keep doing what you've been doing, I wish you the best of luck continuing to grow your business. Just remember to keep donating to the less fortunate.

To those who want to explore creating possibilities and the kind of results you might glean by surrounding yourself with a world-class team whose members think and act like owners, let's talk.

Make it the day you choose it to be!

STUART FRIEDMAN
Long Beach, CA
December, 2023
(312) 543-0013
stuart@leadersdontsolveproblems.com

ABOUT THE AUTHOR

Stuart Friedman is a leadership and business visionary. He works with business owners who want to avoid team malpractice and raise the bar on their own performance. As a master facilitator, he creates experiences where teams solve problems and each member begins to think and act like an owner. He uses the art of provocation to challenge leaders to shift their paradigms and surround themselves with world-class teams.

Stuart...

"...is not your typical consultant or coach. He doesn't just tell you what you want to hear. He is the one person who will tell you the truth, what you *need* to hear, and hold you accountable."
— *David M., Owner/CEO, Manufacturing*

"...brings a no-nonsense approach, with simple applications to help align people and roles. His keen assessments enable us to better discern who is right for our team and culture."
— *Richard D., Principal, Asset Management Company*

"...is an expert at helping owners assess issues and barriers that are affecting individual and team performance. He gets people at all levels of an organization talking, thinking, and acting like owners."

    – Carol R., Owner, Insurance

"...understands what it means to be a CEO or owner. He can help you optimize on your constraints and understand how your team can best work and communicate to achieve goals."

    – Donna B., President/CEO, Technology Company

"...worked with me and my 15-person leadership team for several years. We went from losing $1 million/year to making a profit of $3 million in just a few years."

    – Jason M., Owner, Transportation/Logistics

"...helped me address one of my biggest challenges as president and CEO, which is to create alignment with my team and to mobilize them."

    – Dennis A., President, Foodservice Industry

"...understands that when you run a business based on numbers alone, failure is guaranteed. What's important are the *people* involved and whether they're excited to be on the job every day."

    – Joanne B., CEO, Construction Company

"...provides wisdom, guidance and support that is always appreciated. I am thankful for his overall candid approach with me and genuinely showing how much he wants us to succeed. His approach with the proper tools, strategies, etc., is magical."

    – Sonny R., Co-Founder, EPA Engineering Firm